The Coloring Space

Underwater Kingdoms

Cinzia Sileo

Little, Brown and Company
New York Boston

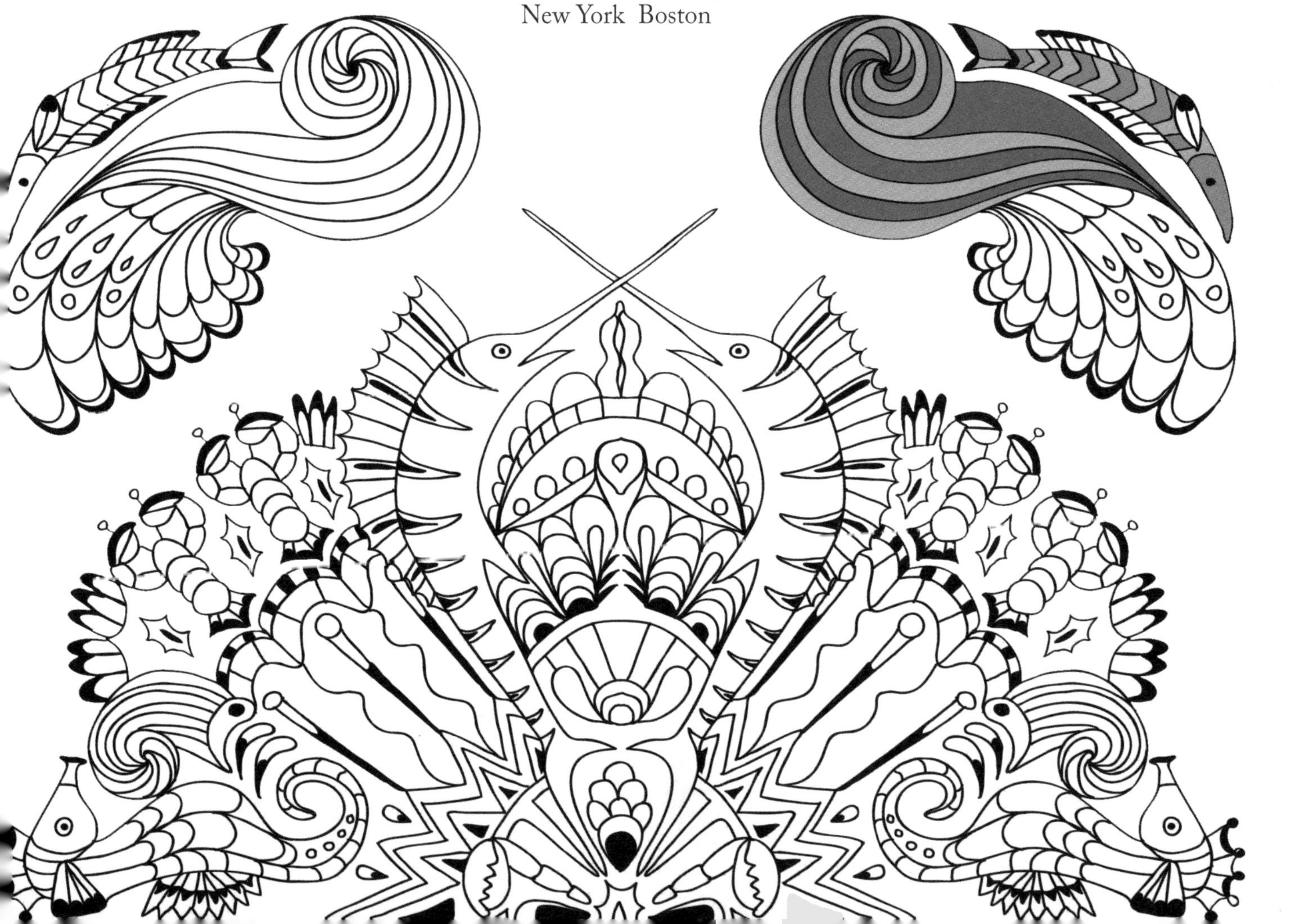

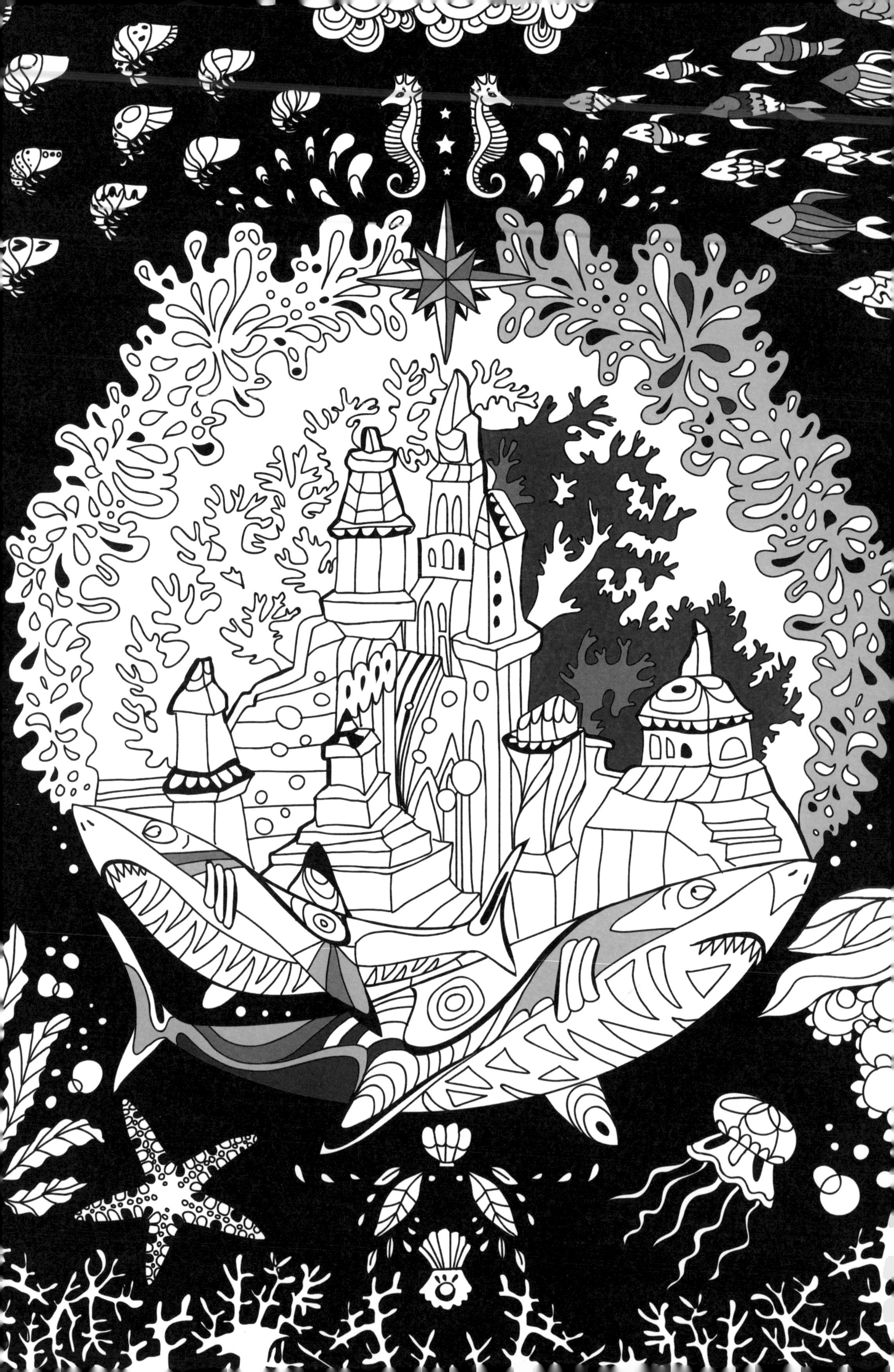

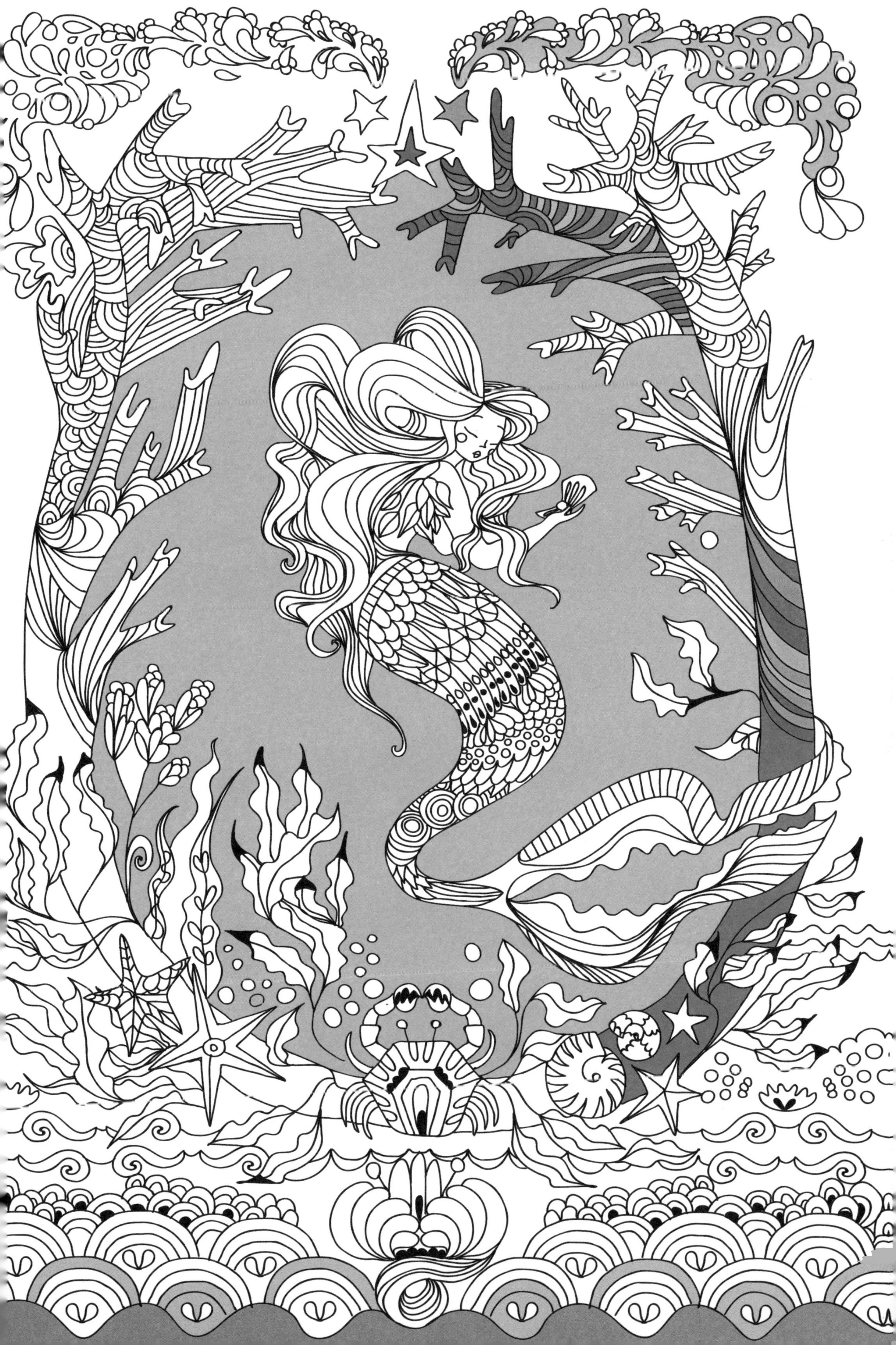

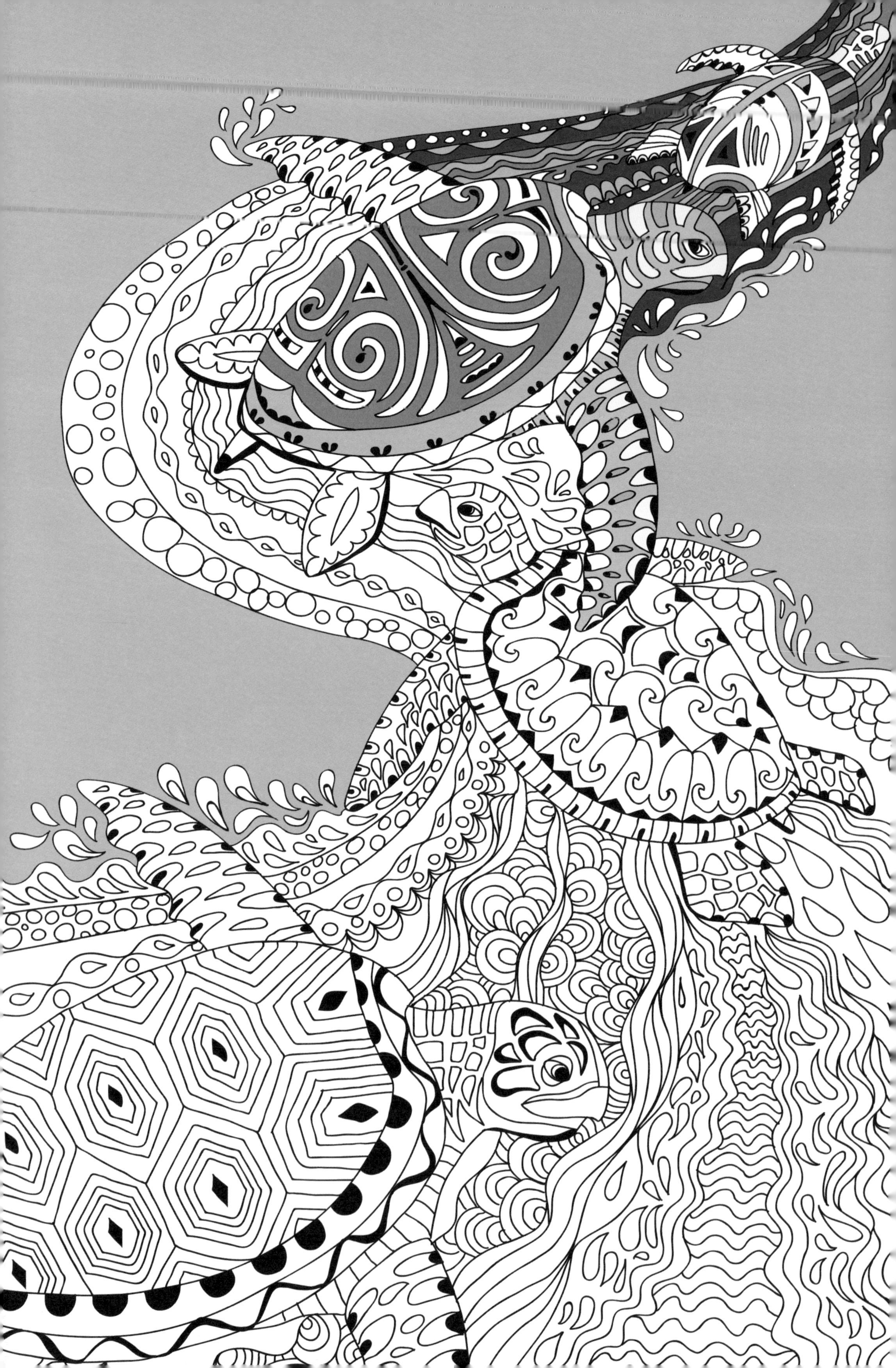

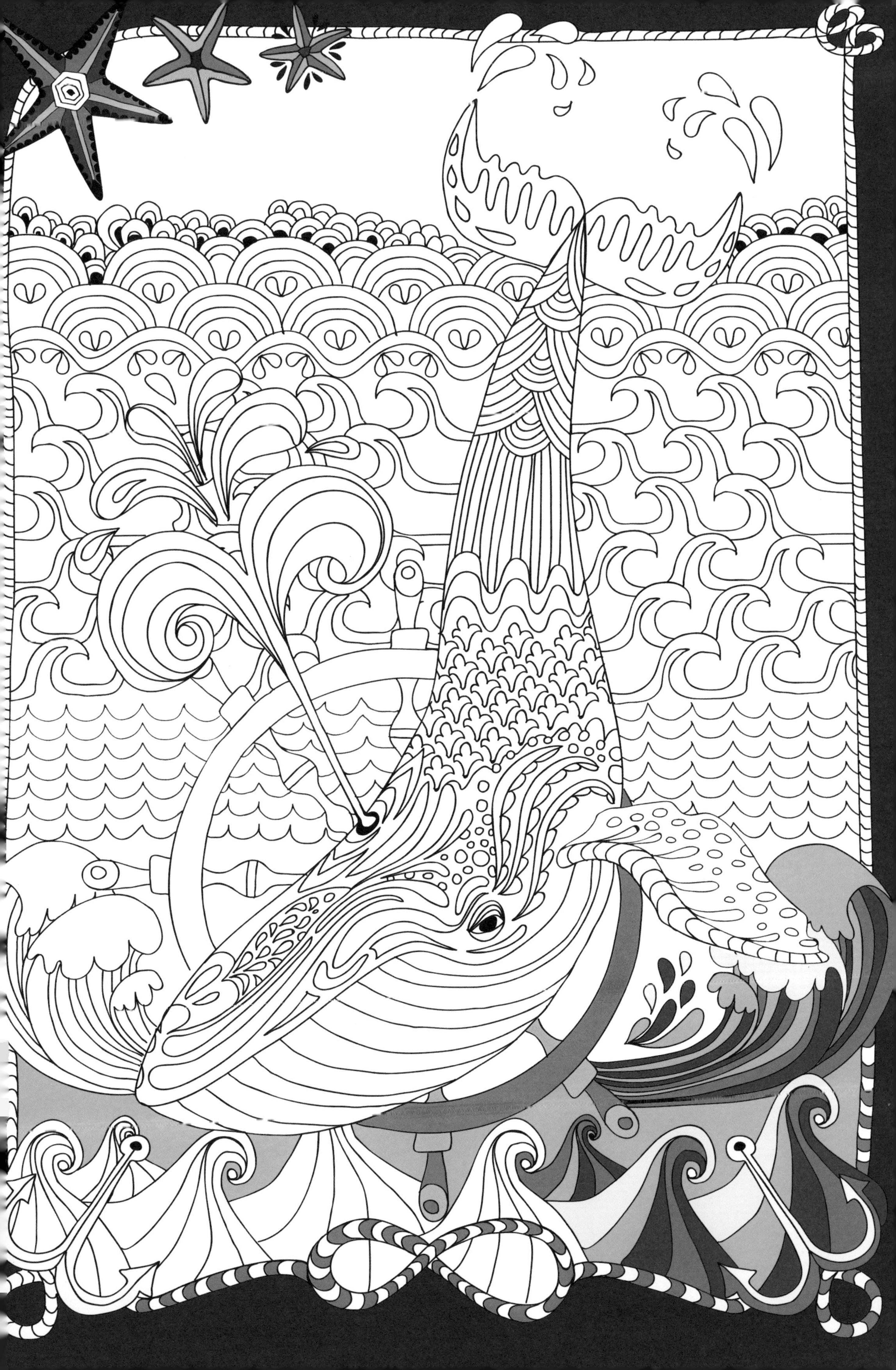

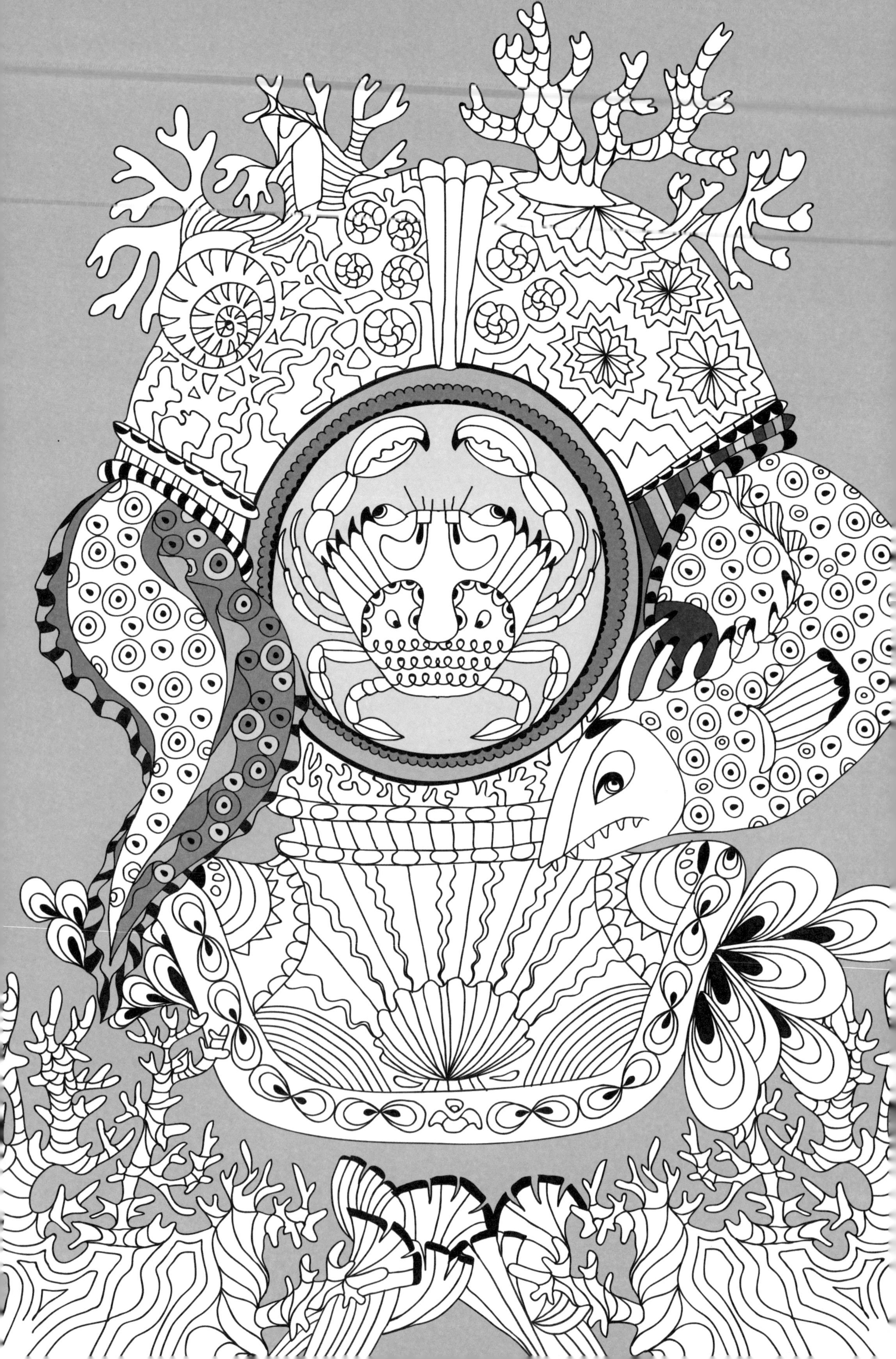

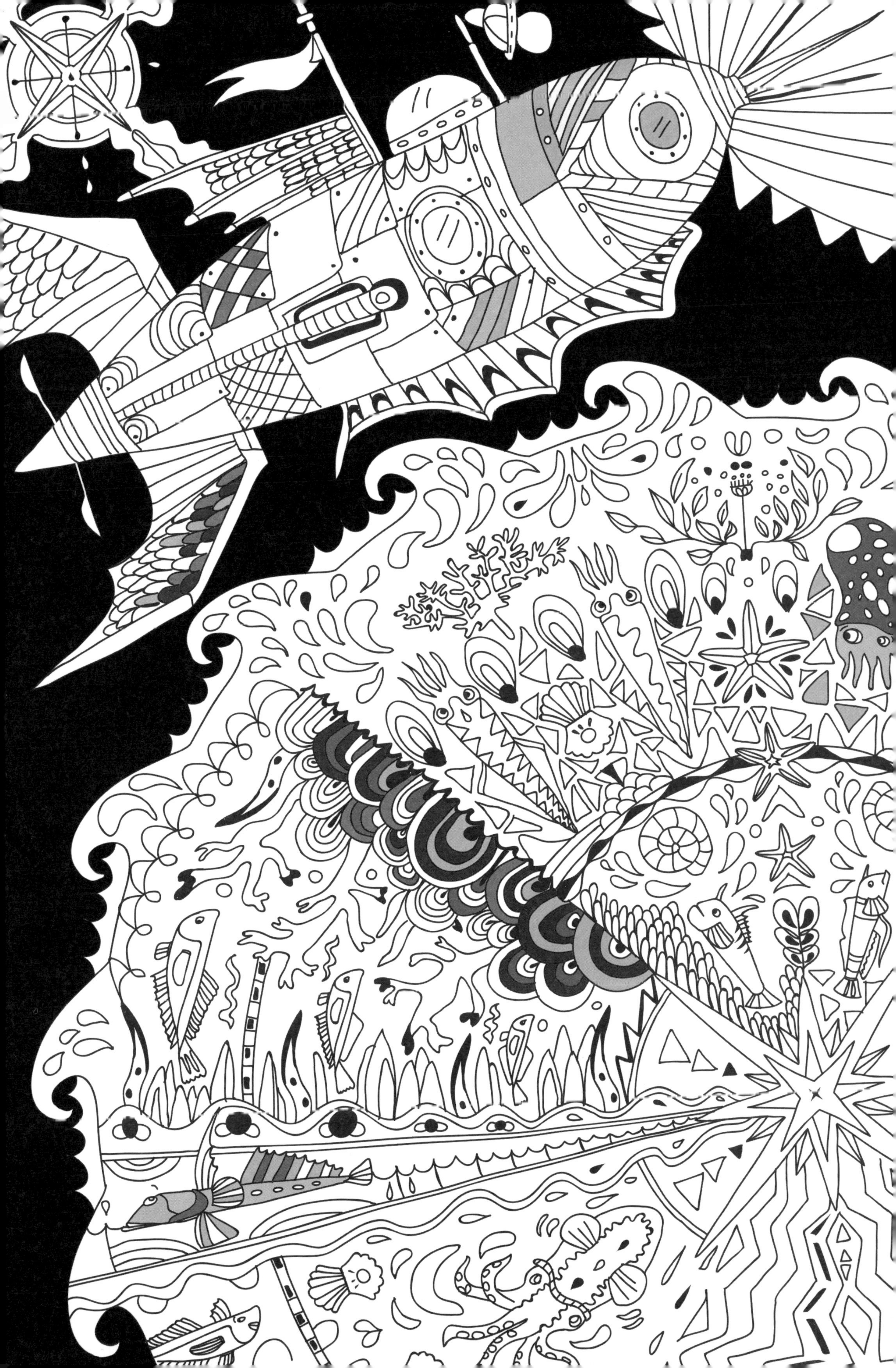

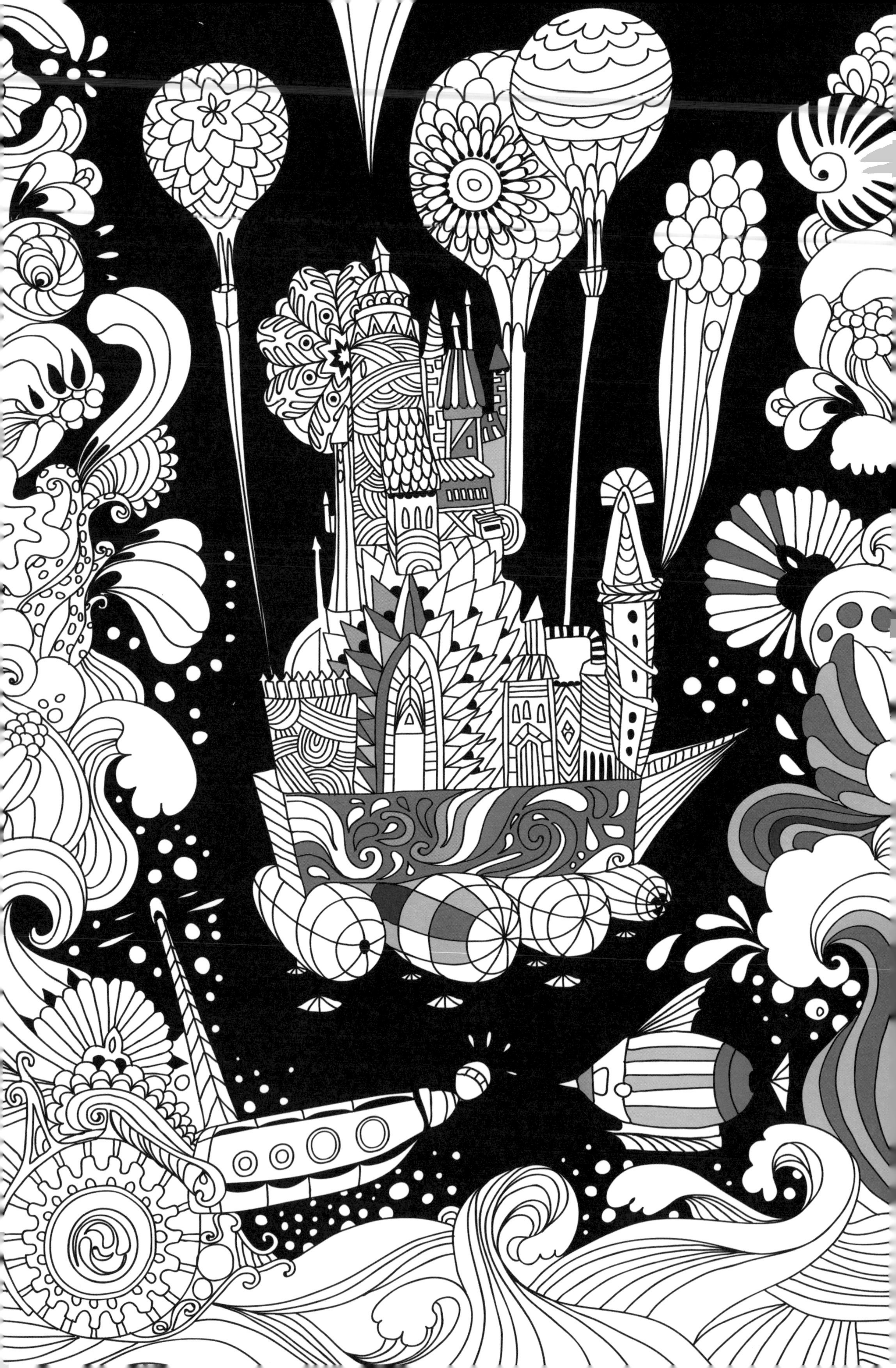

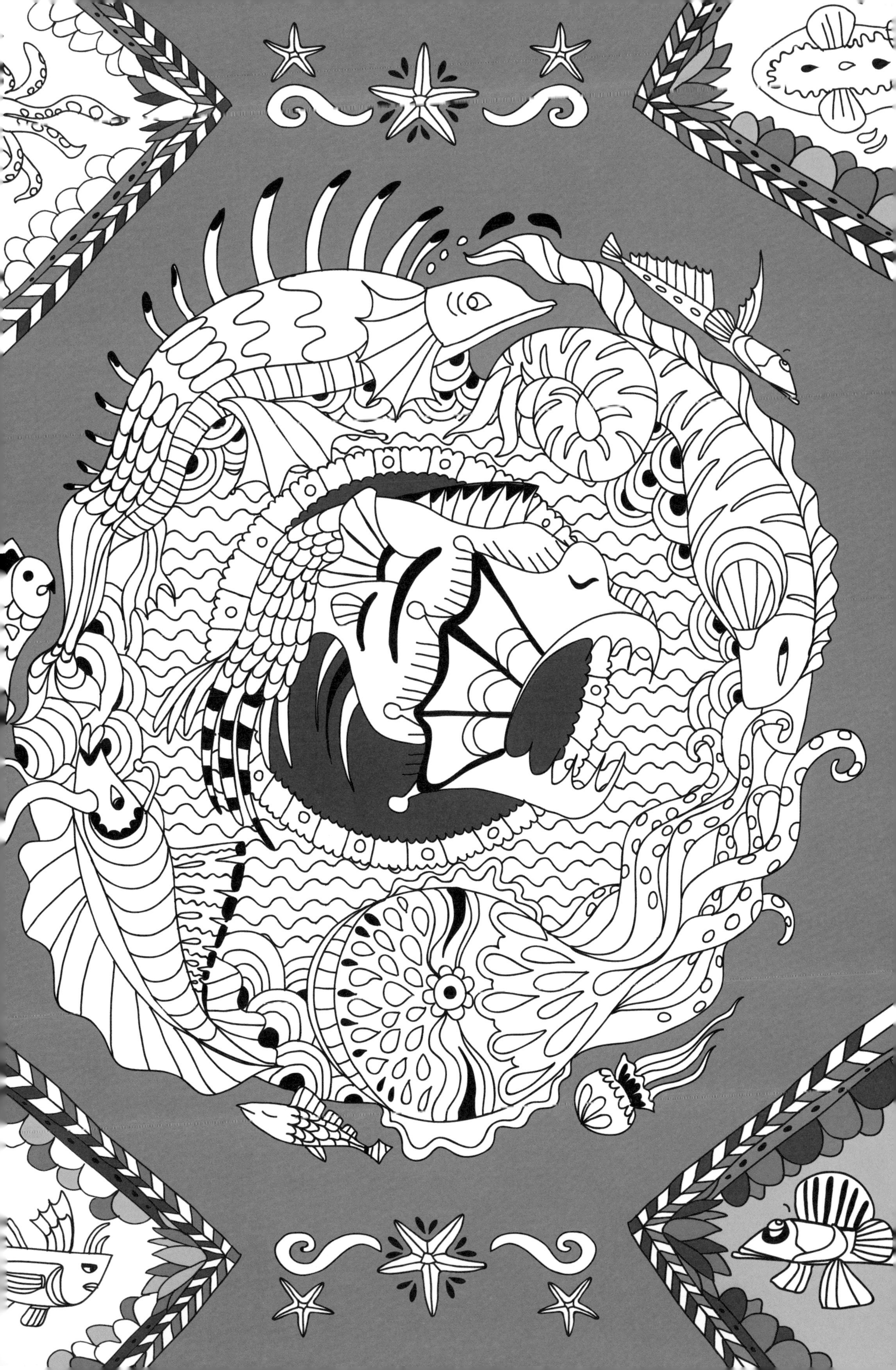

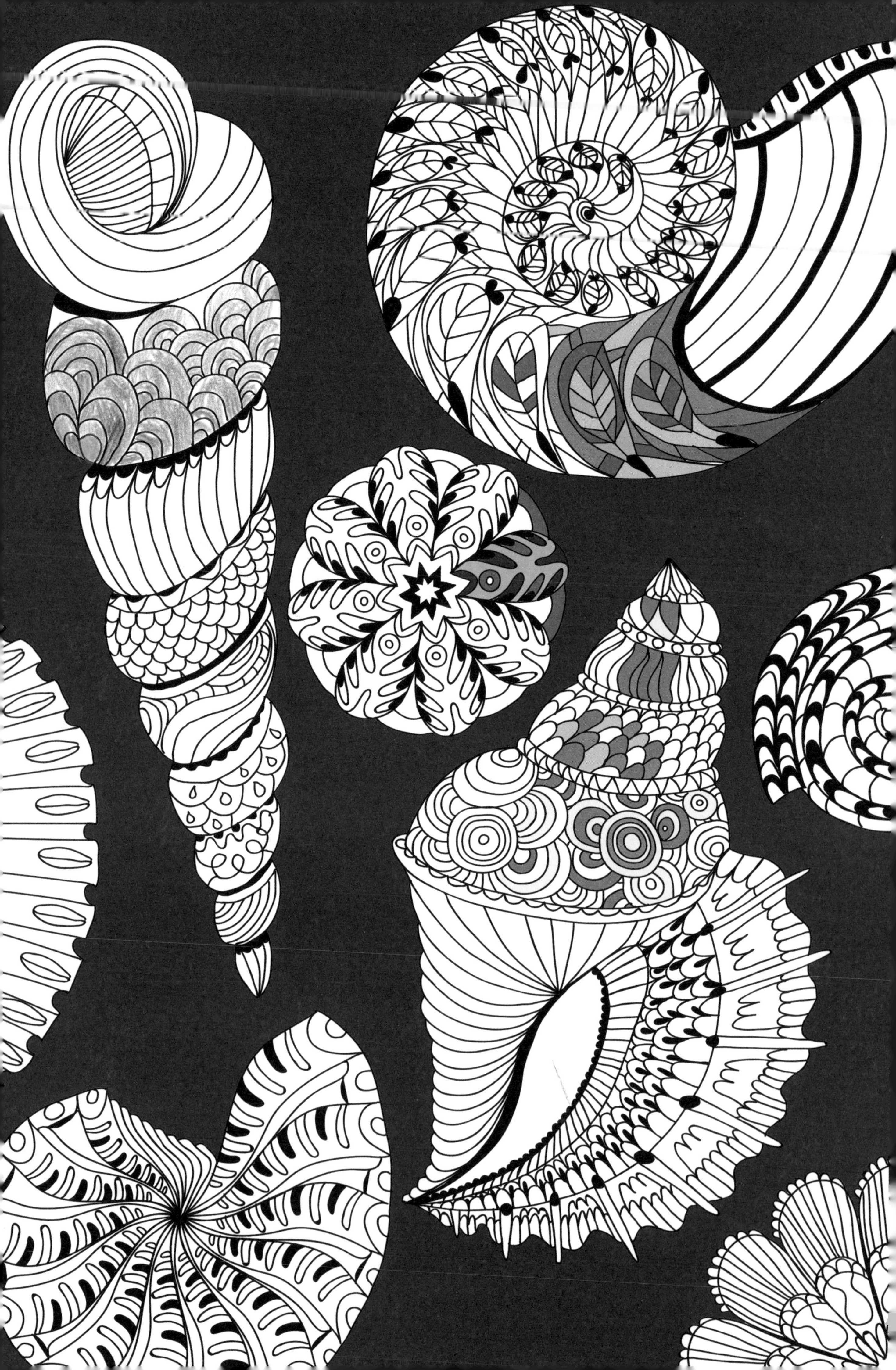

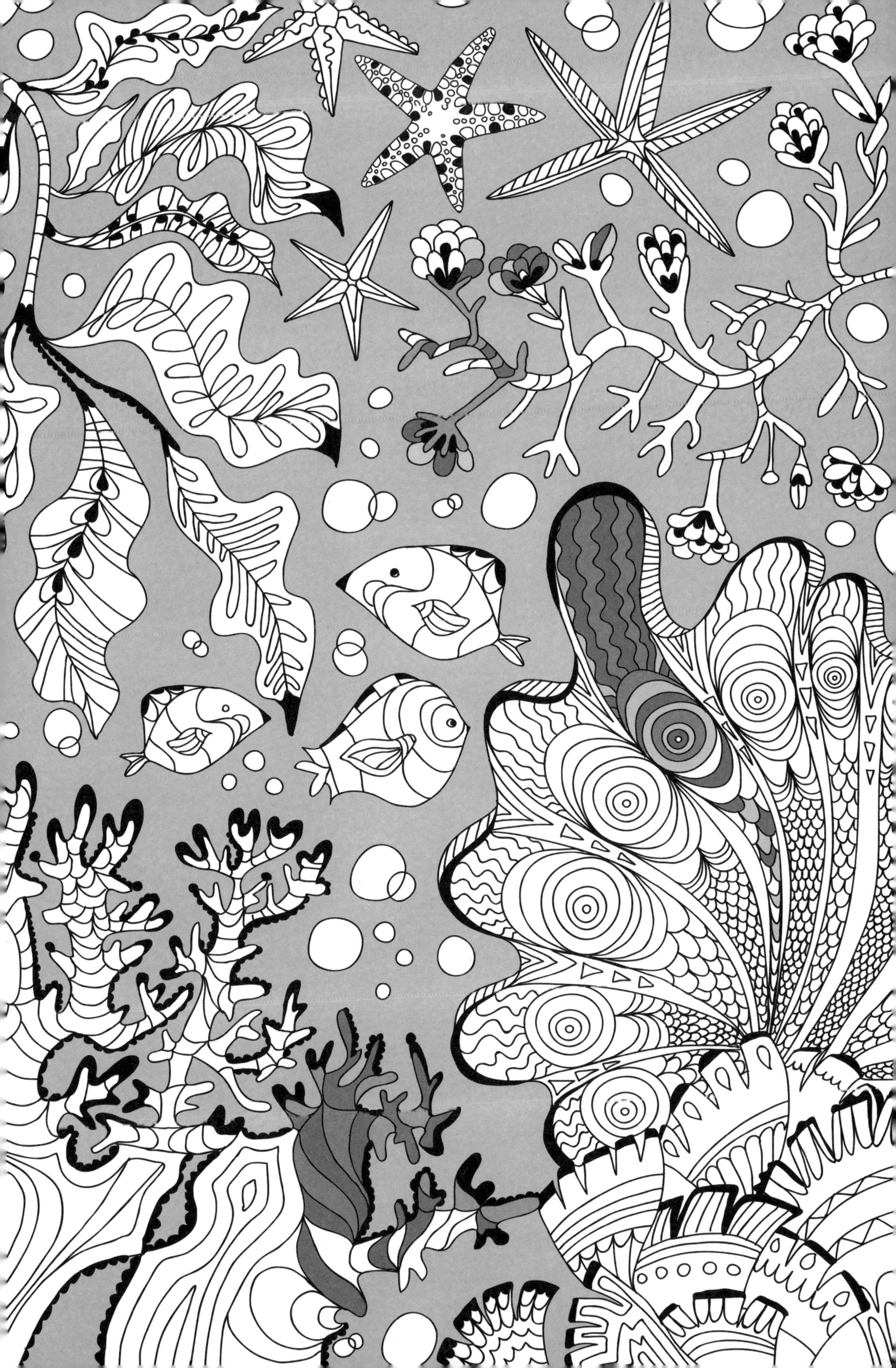

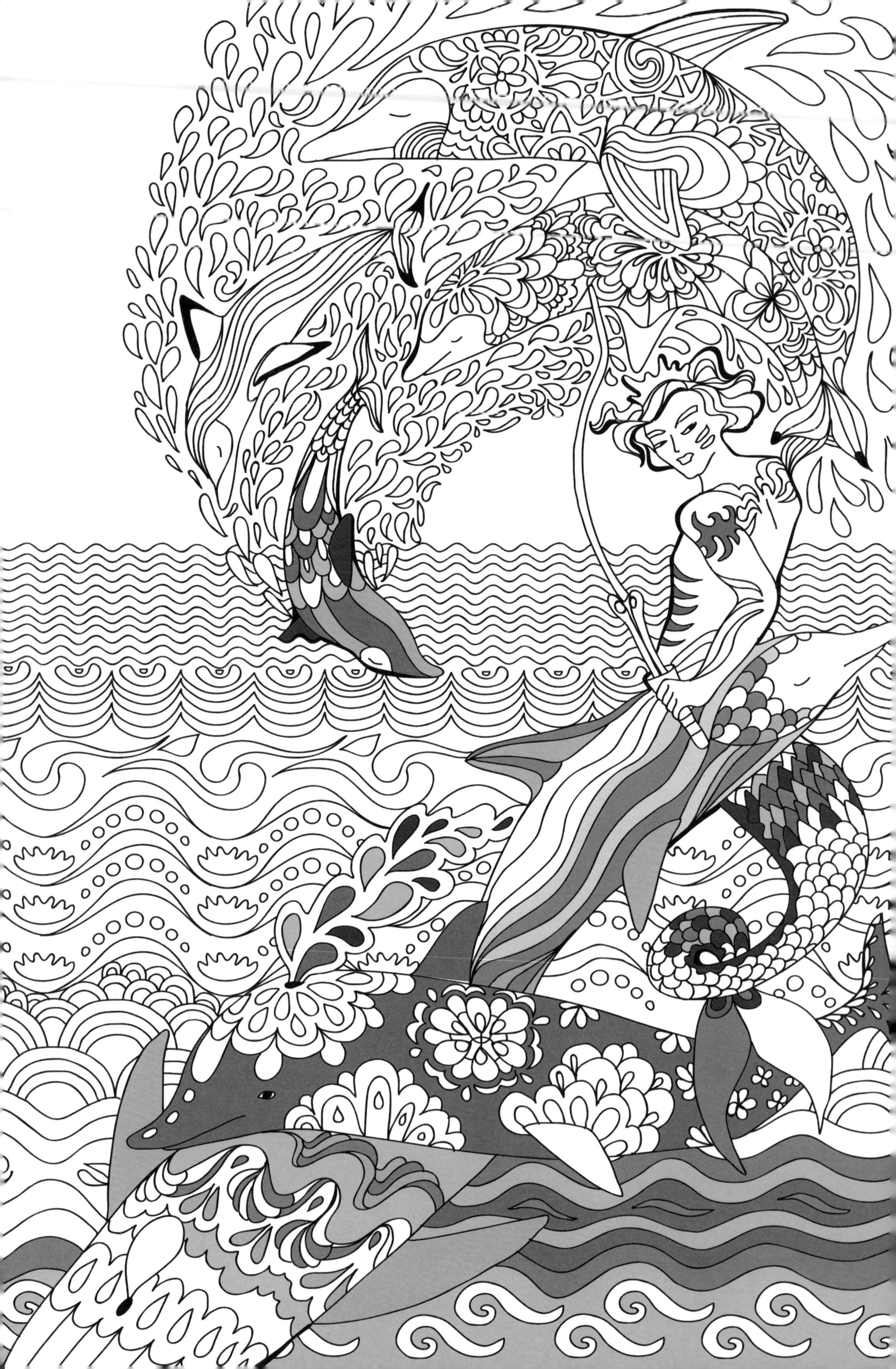

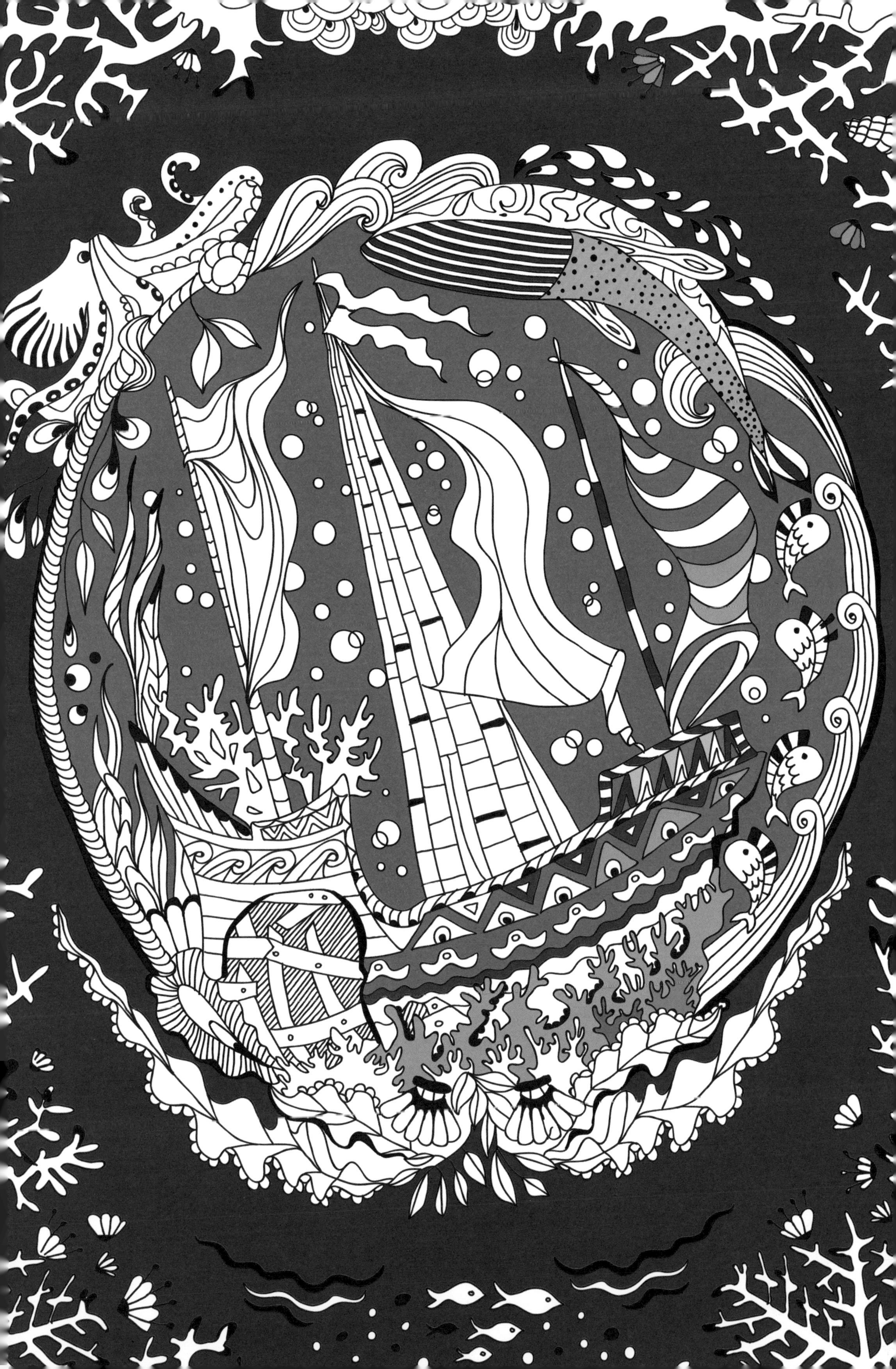

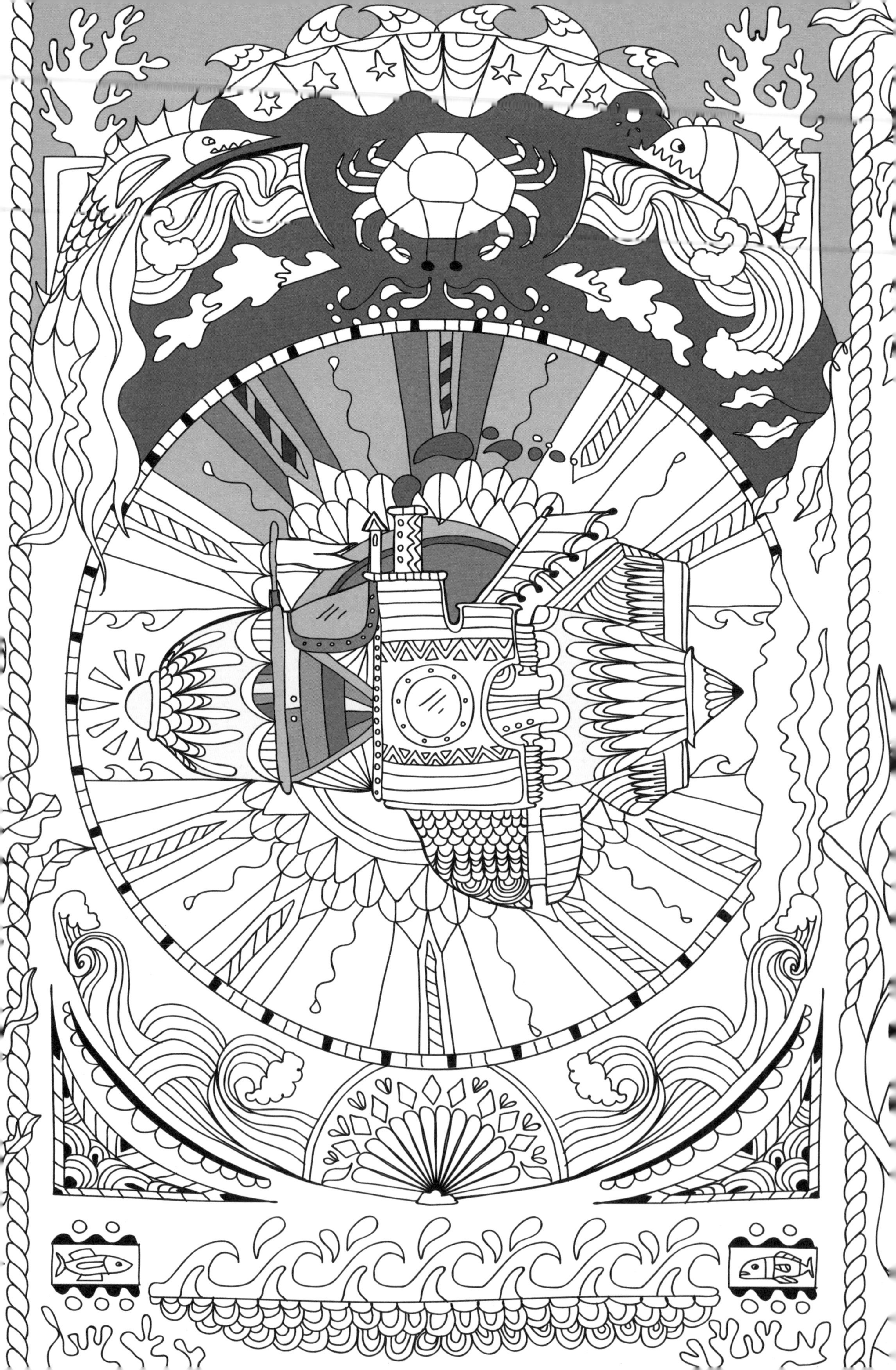

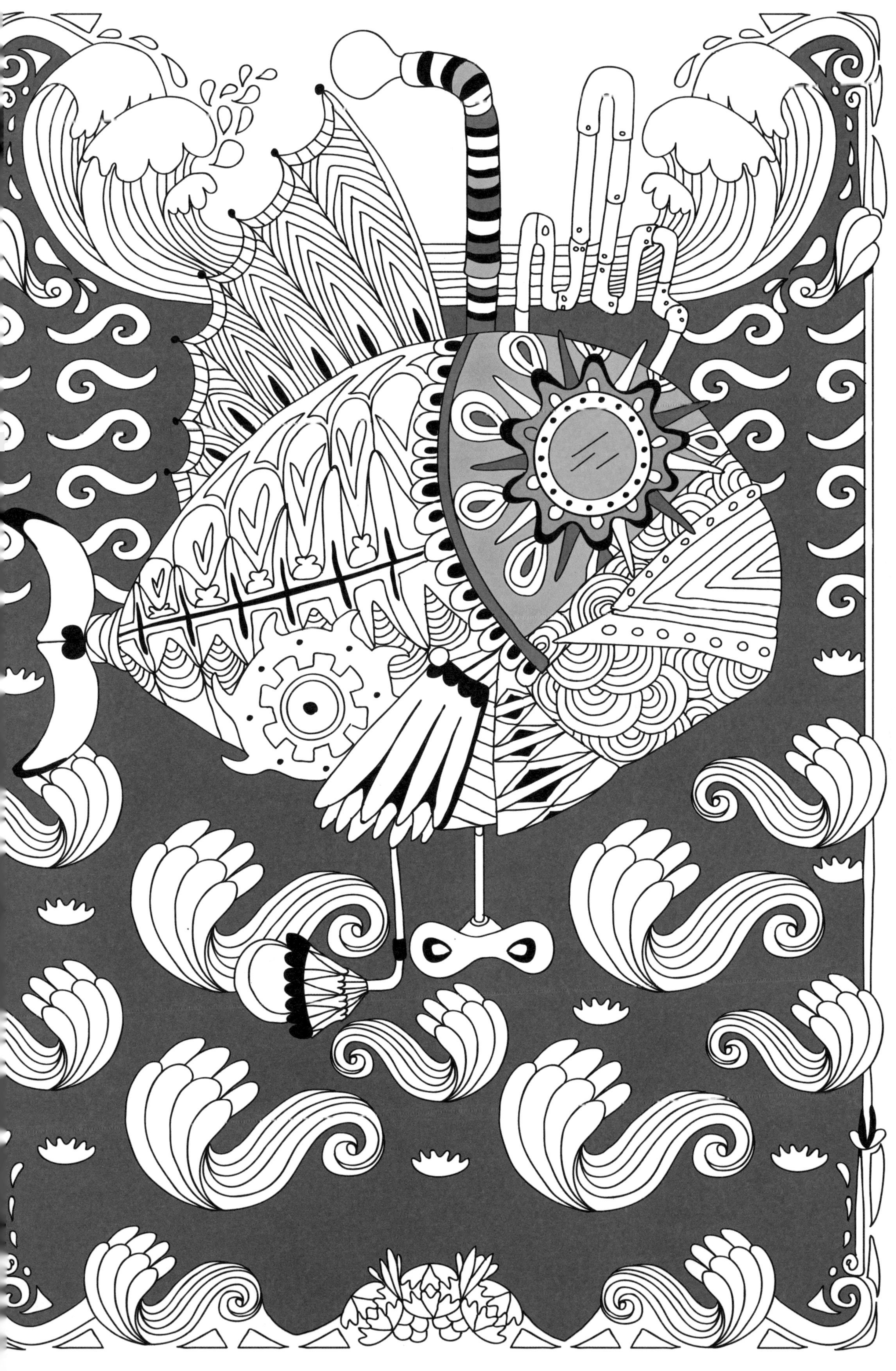

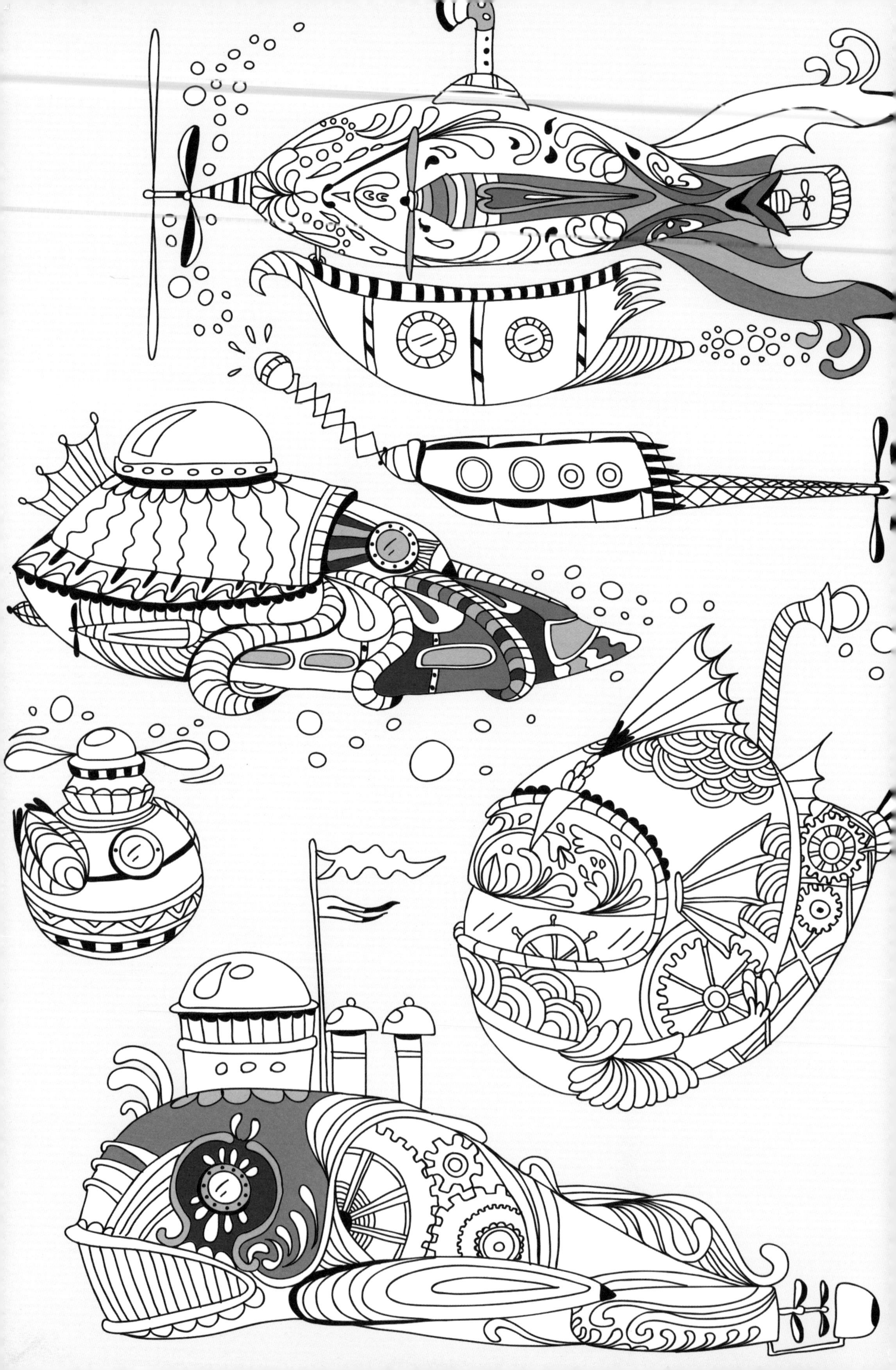

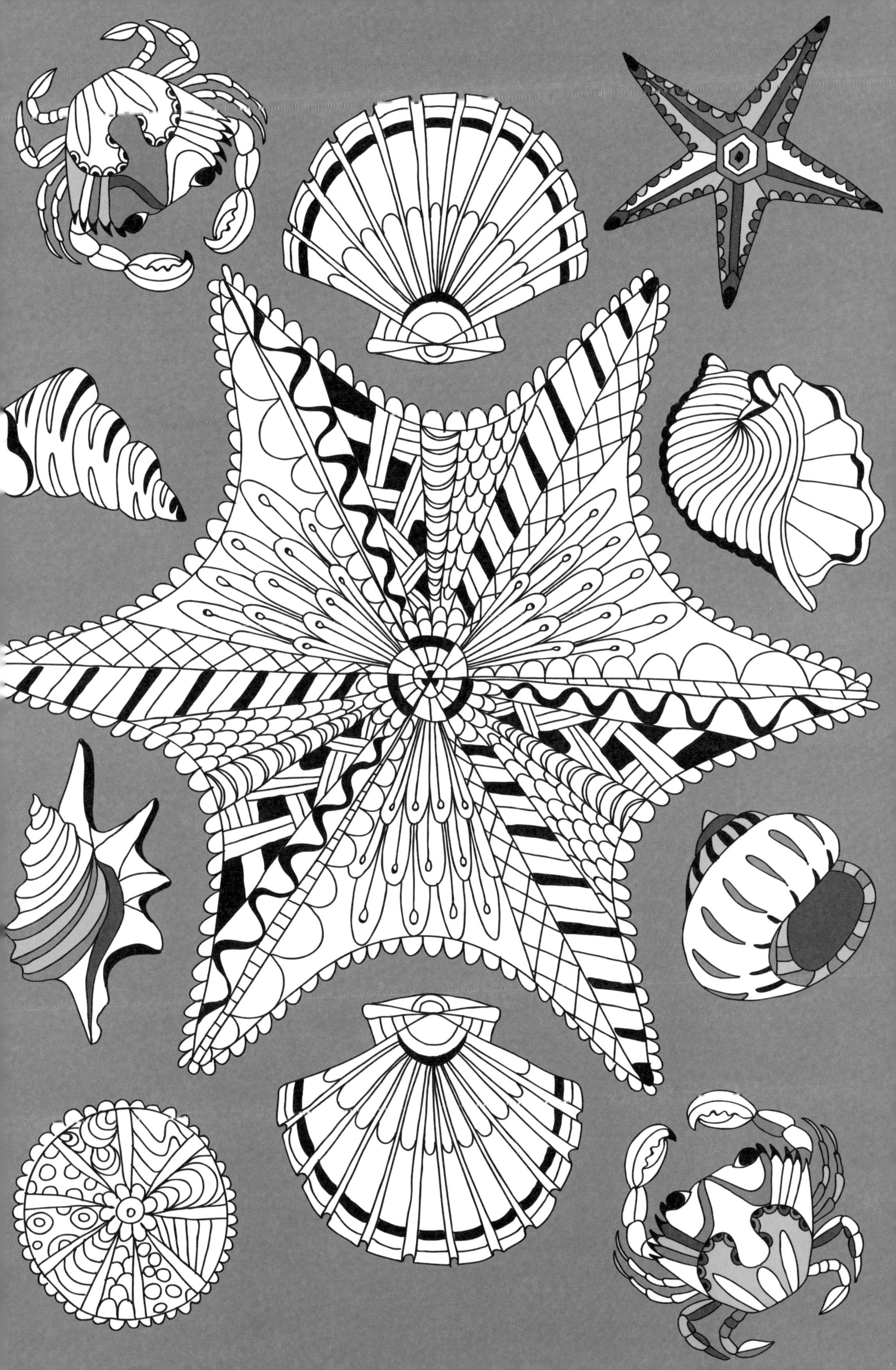

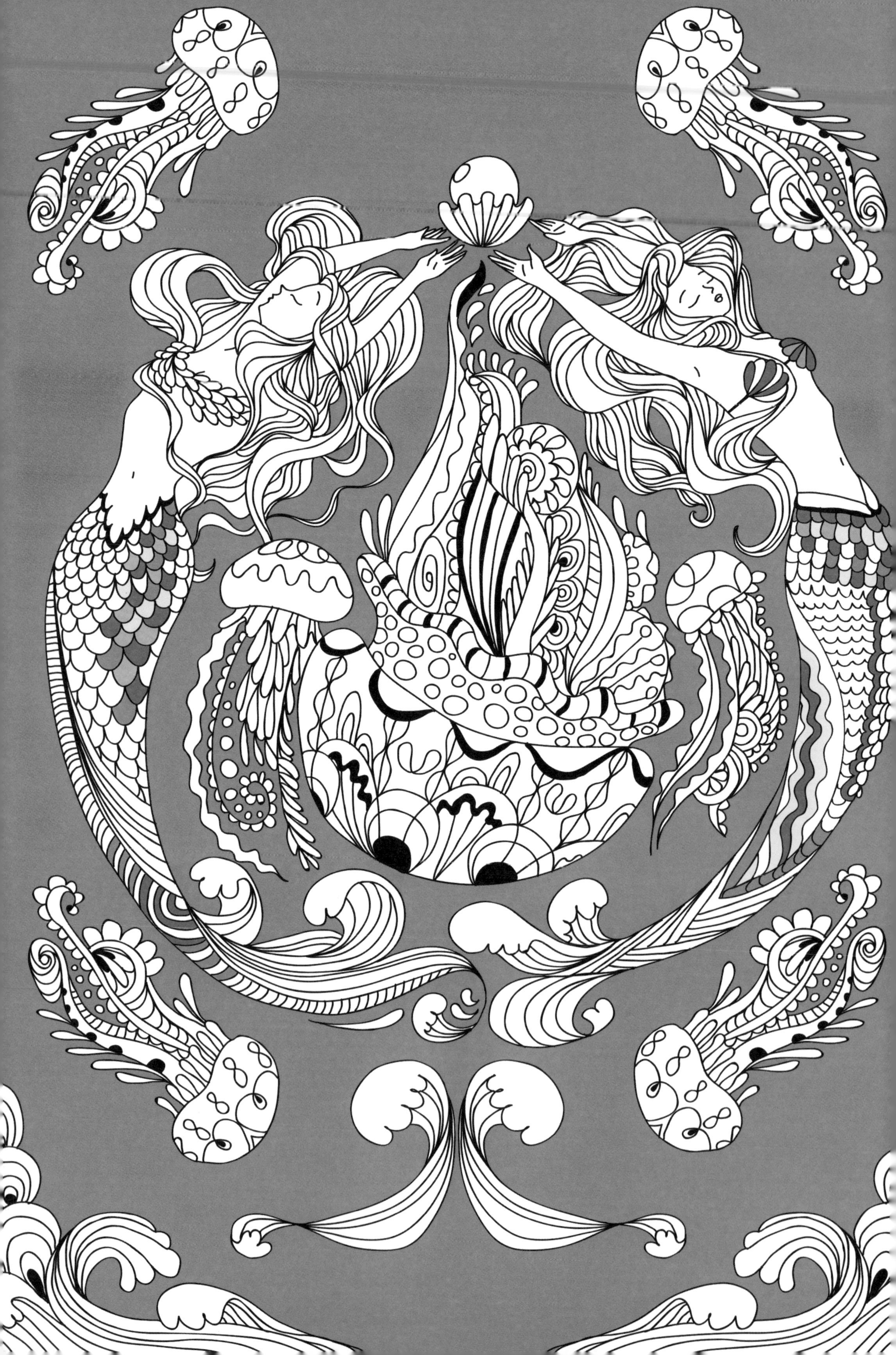

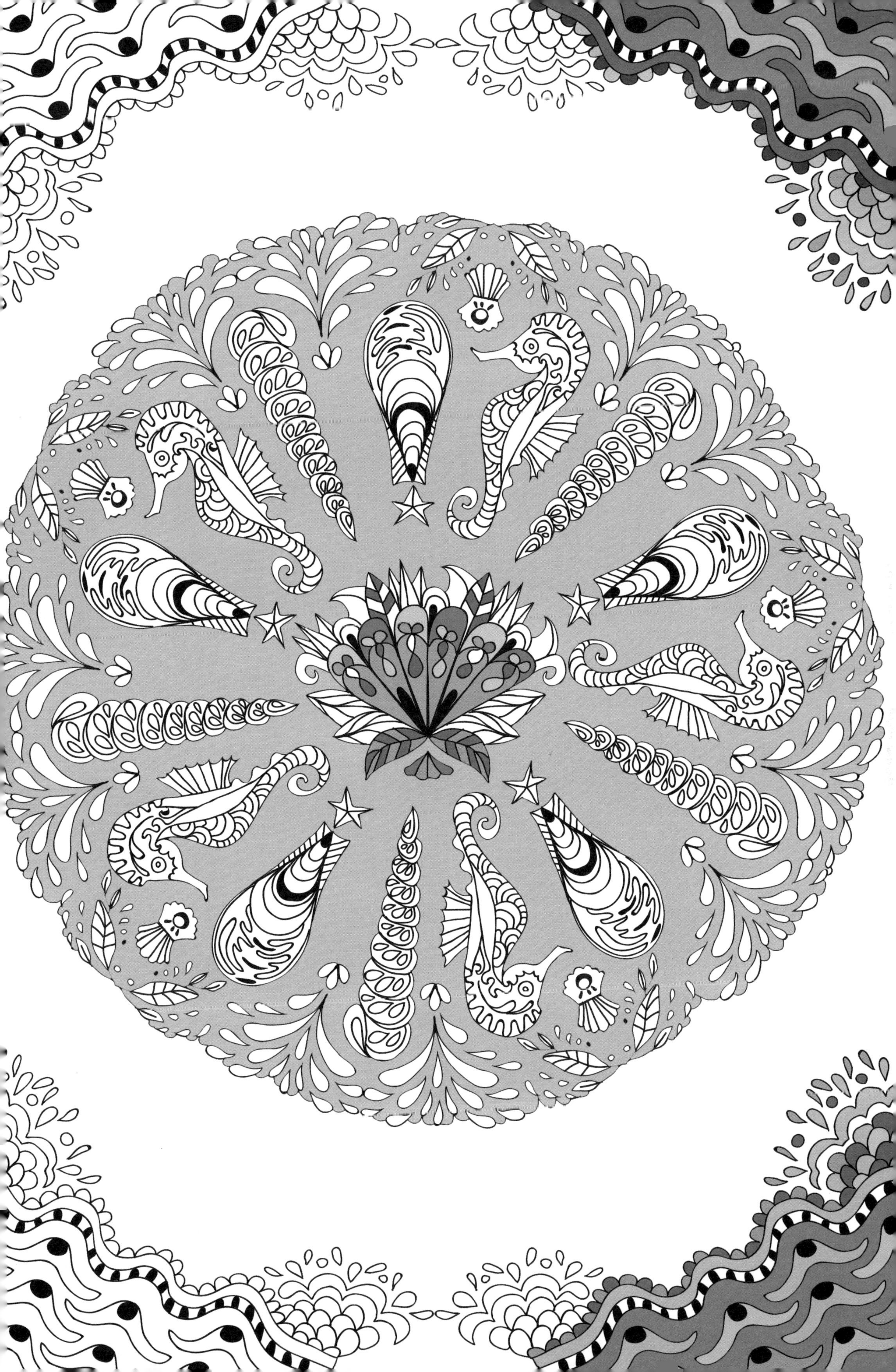

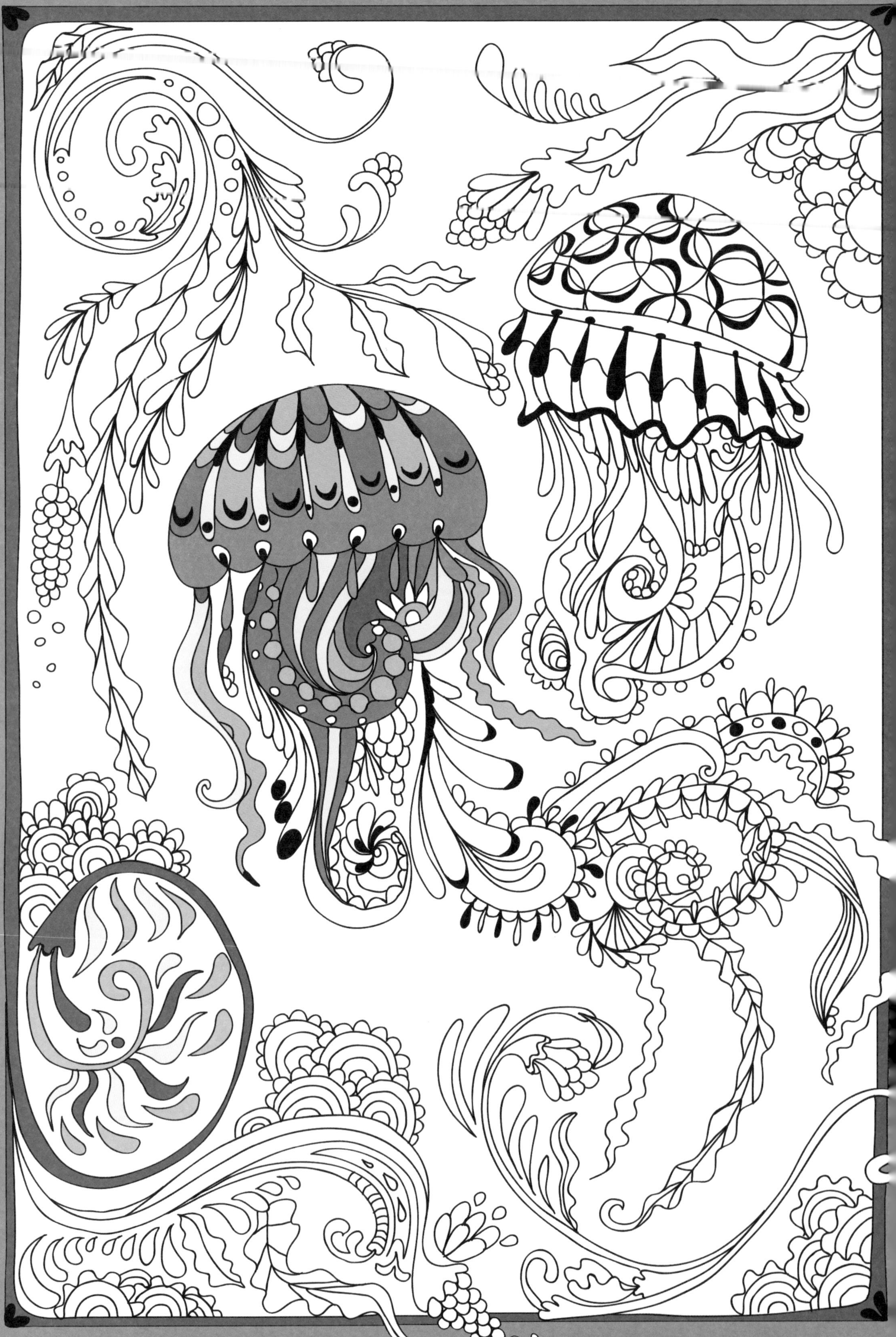

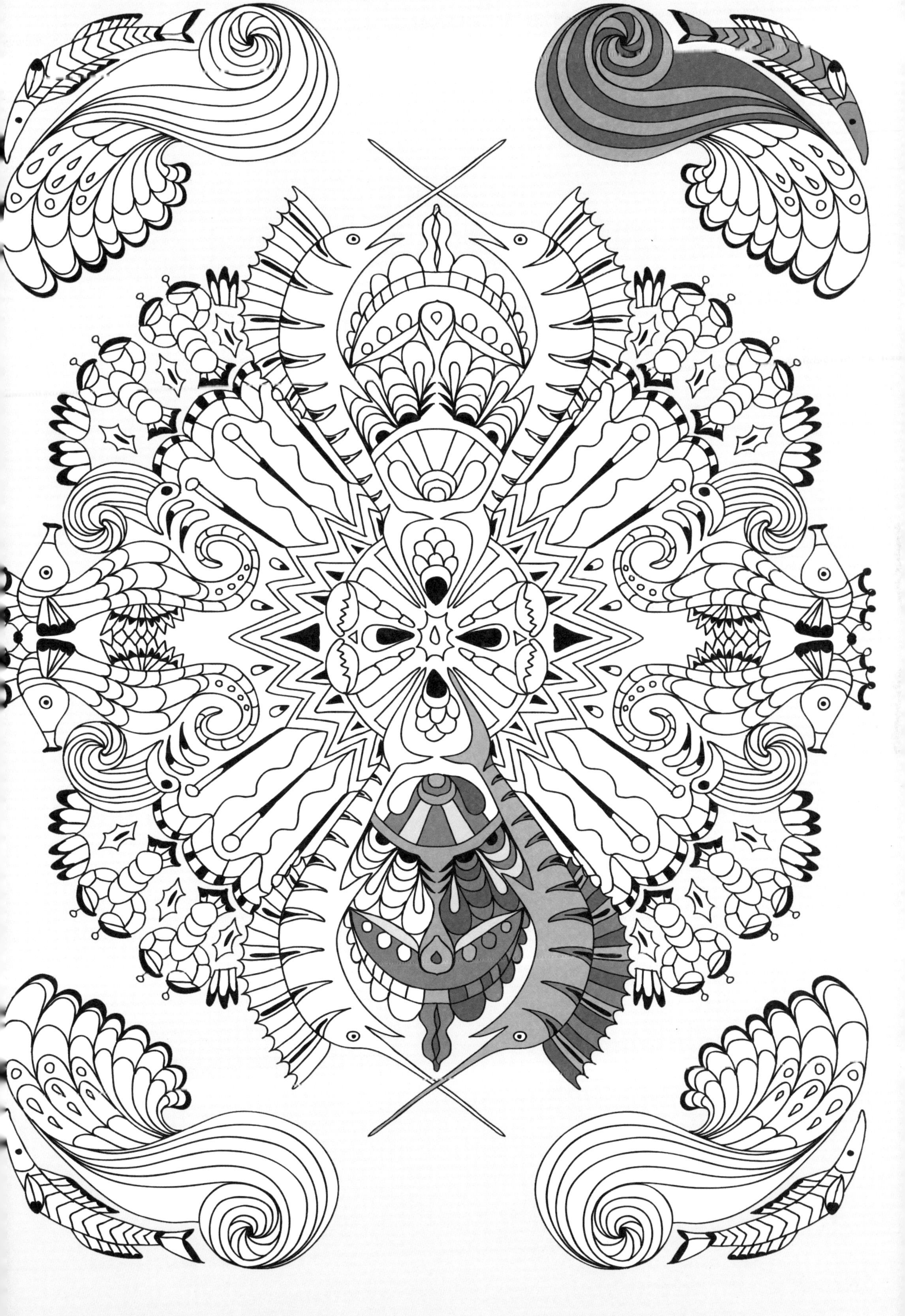

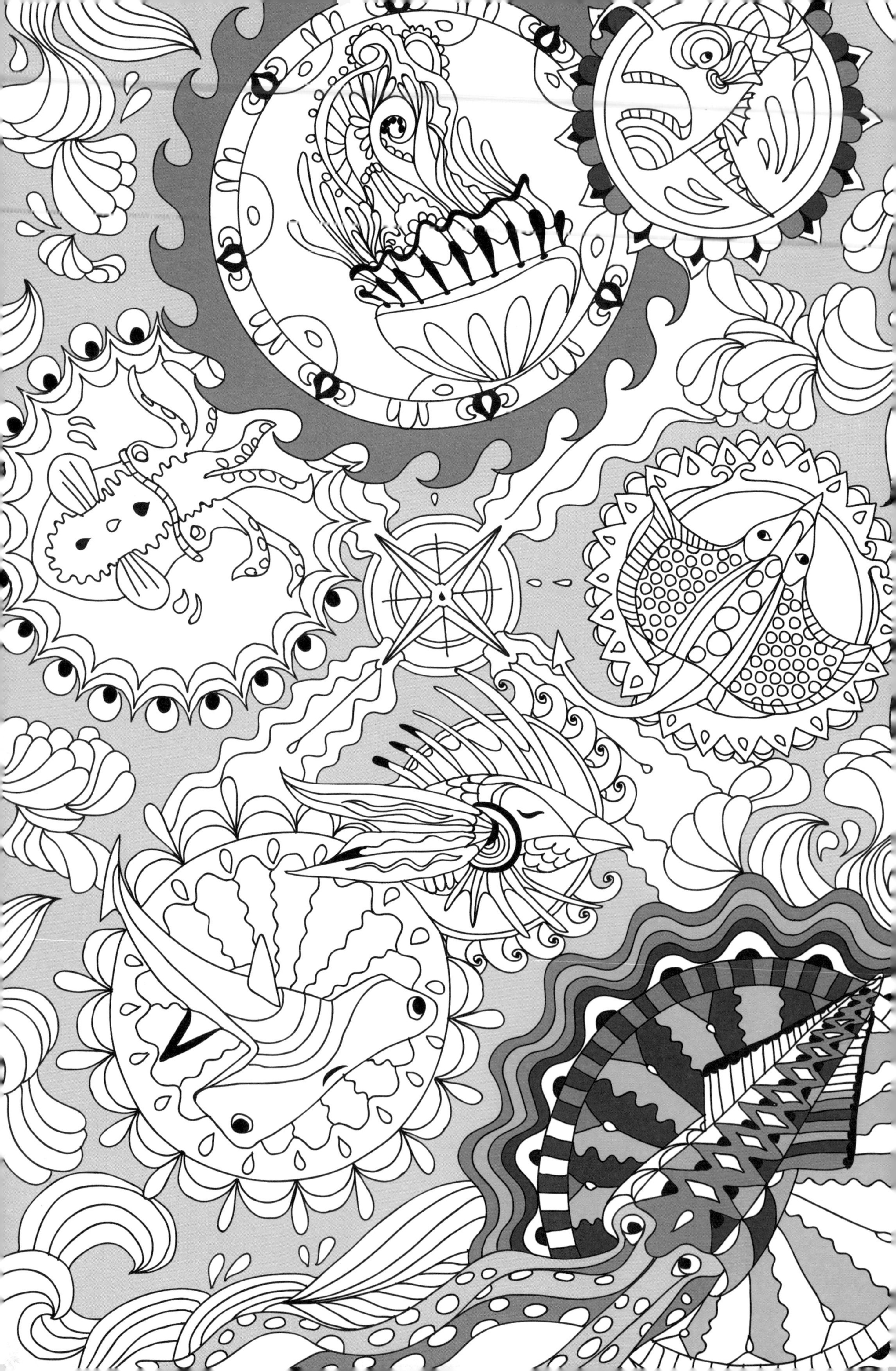

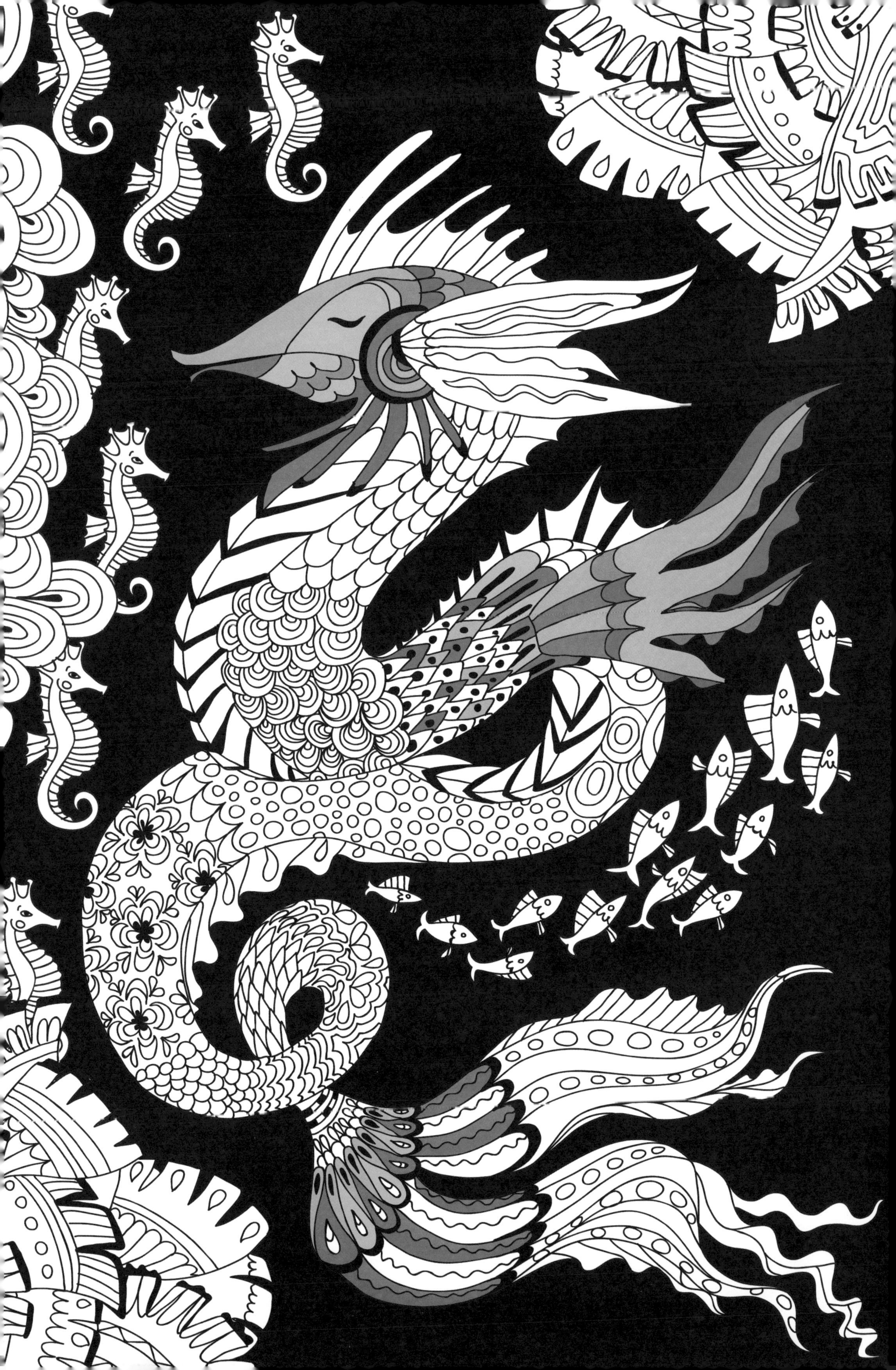

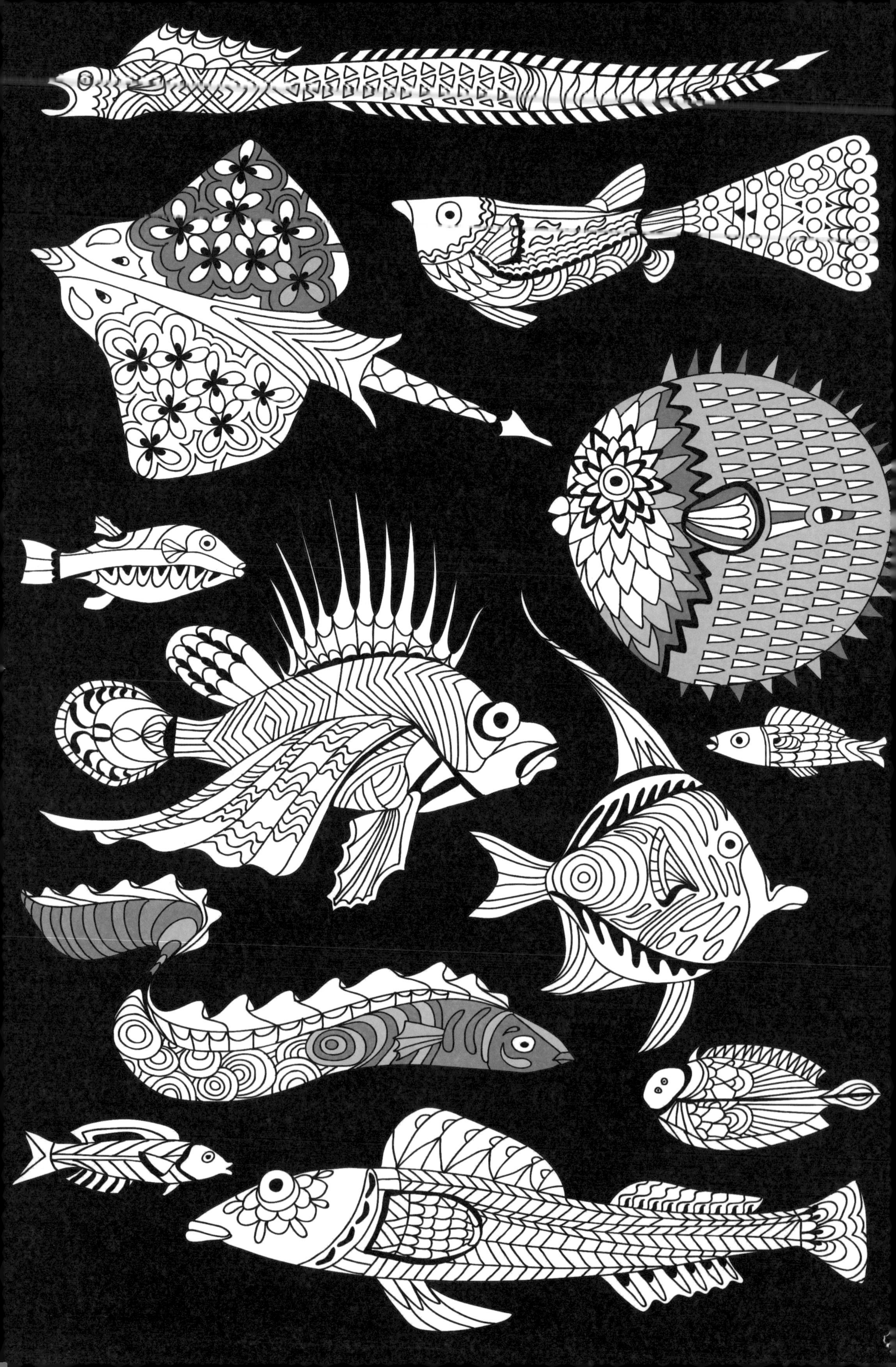

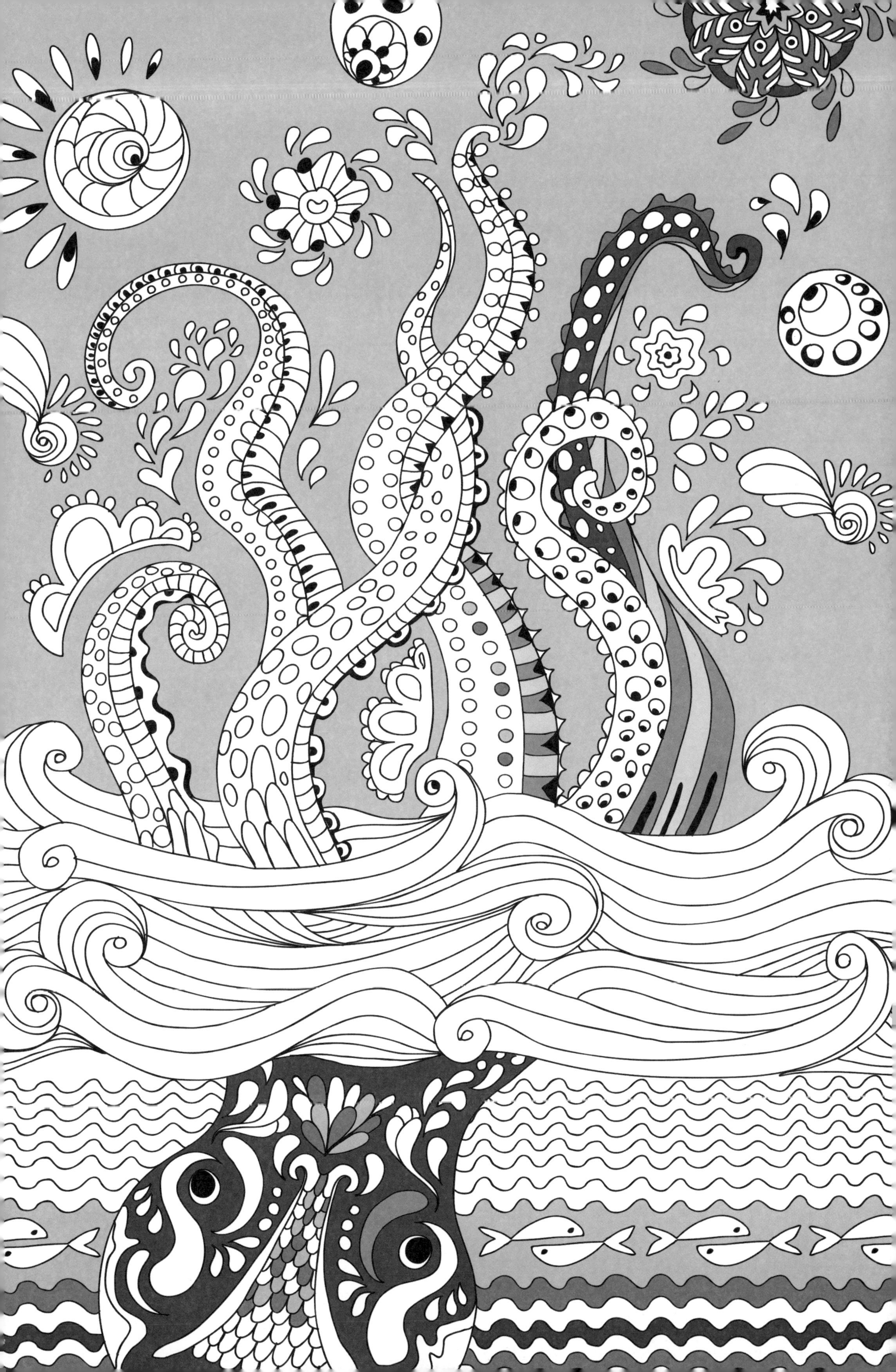

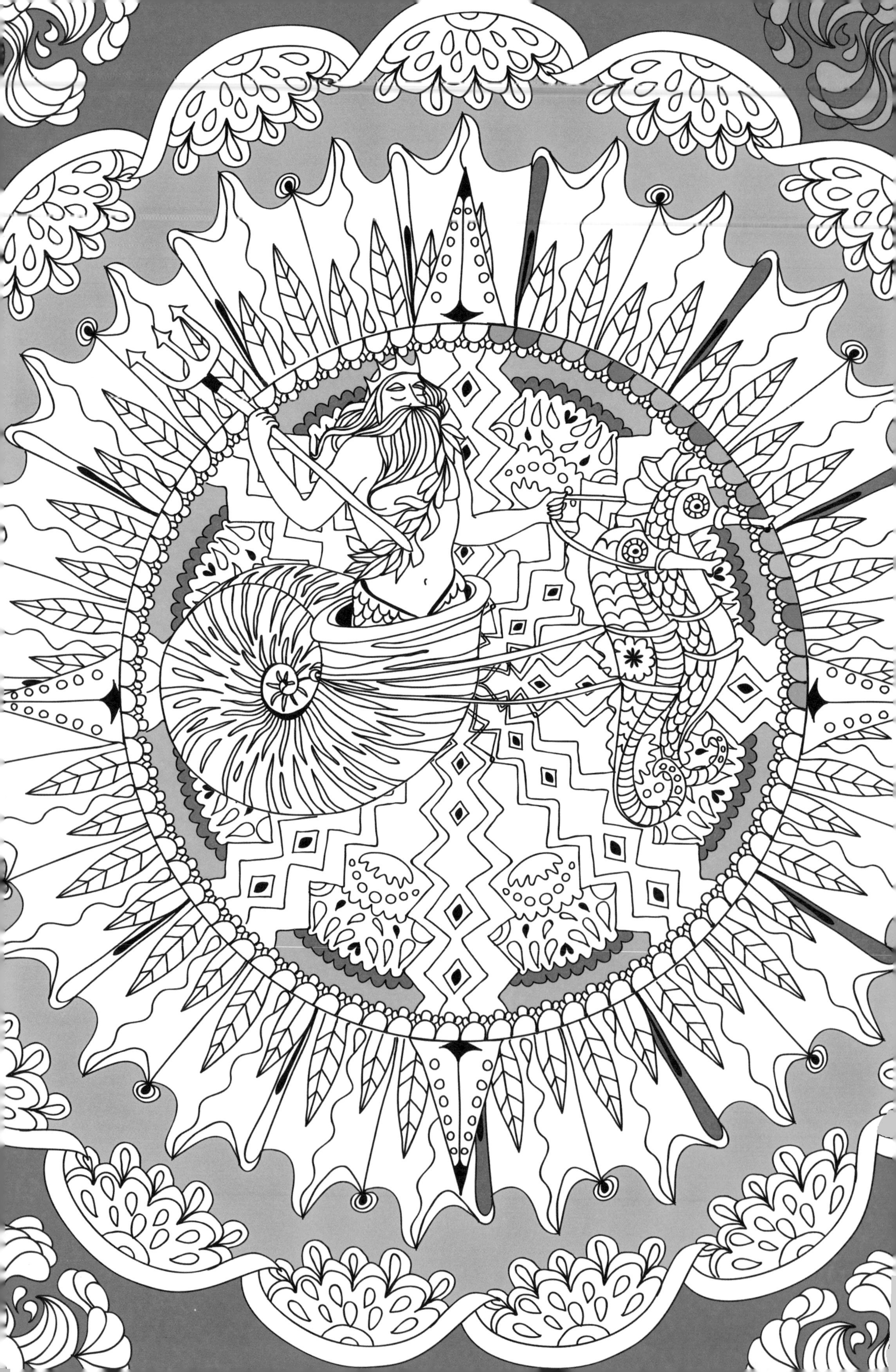

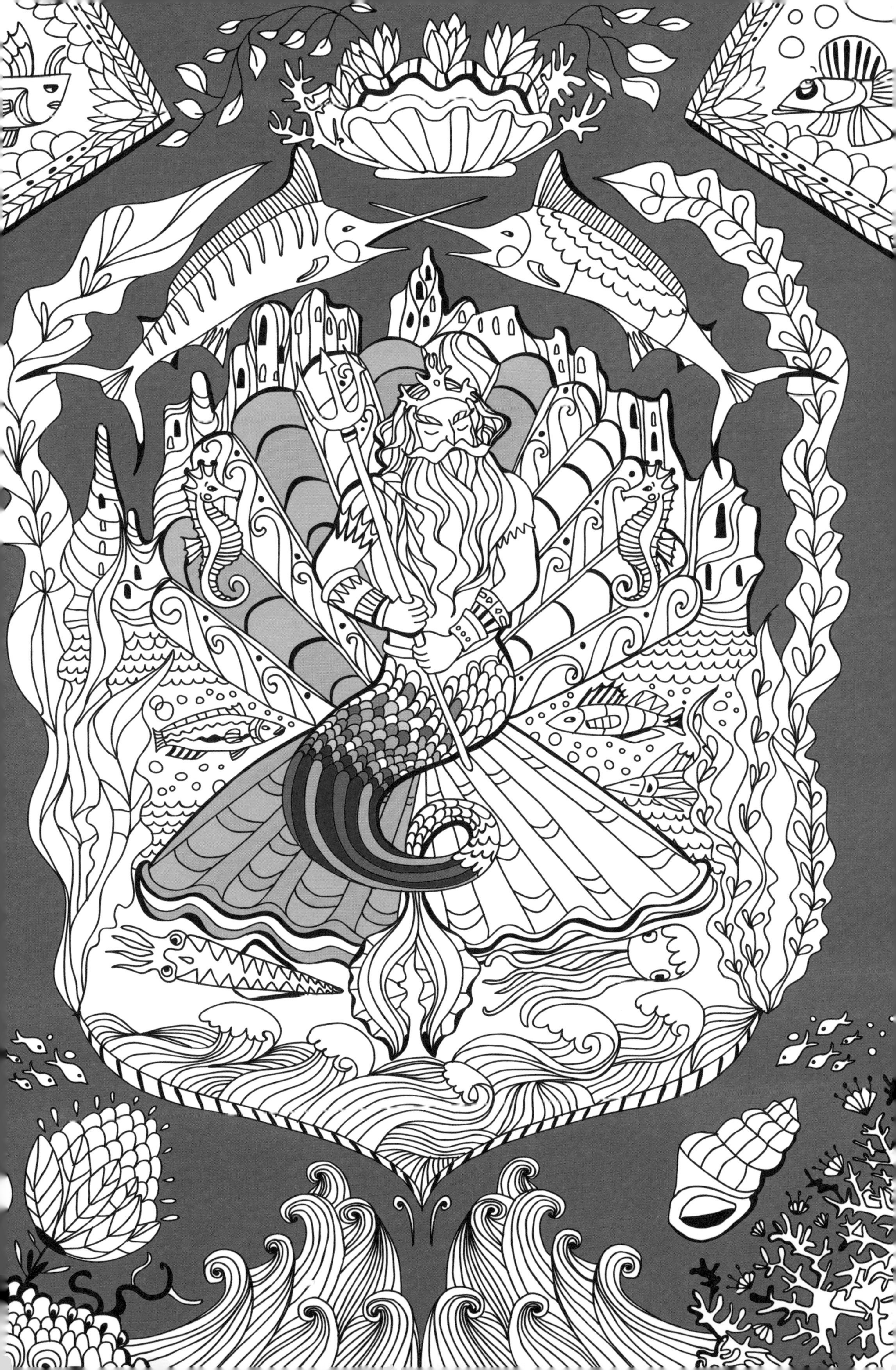

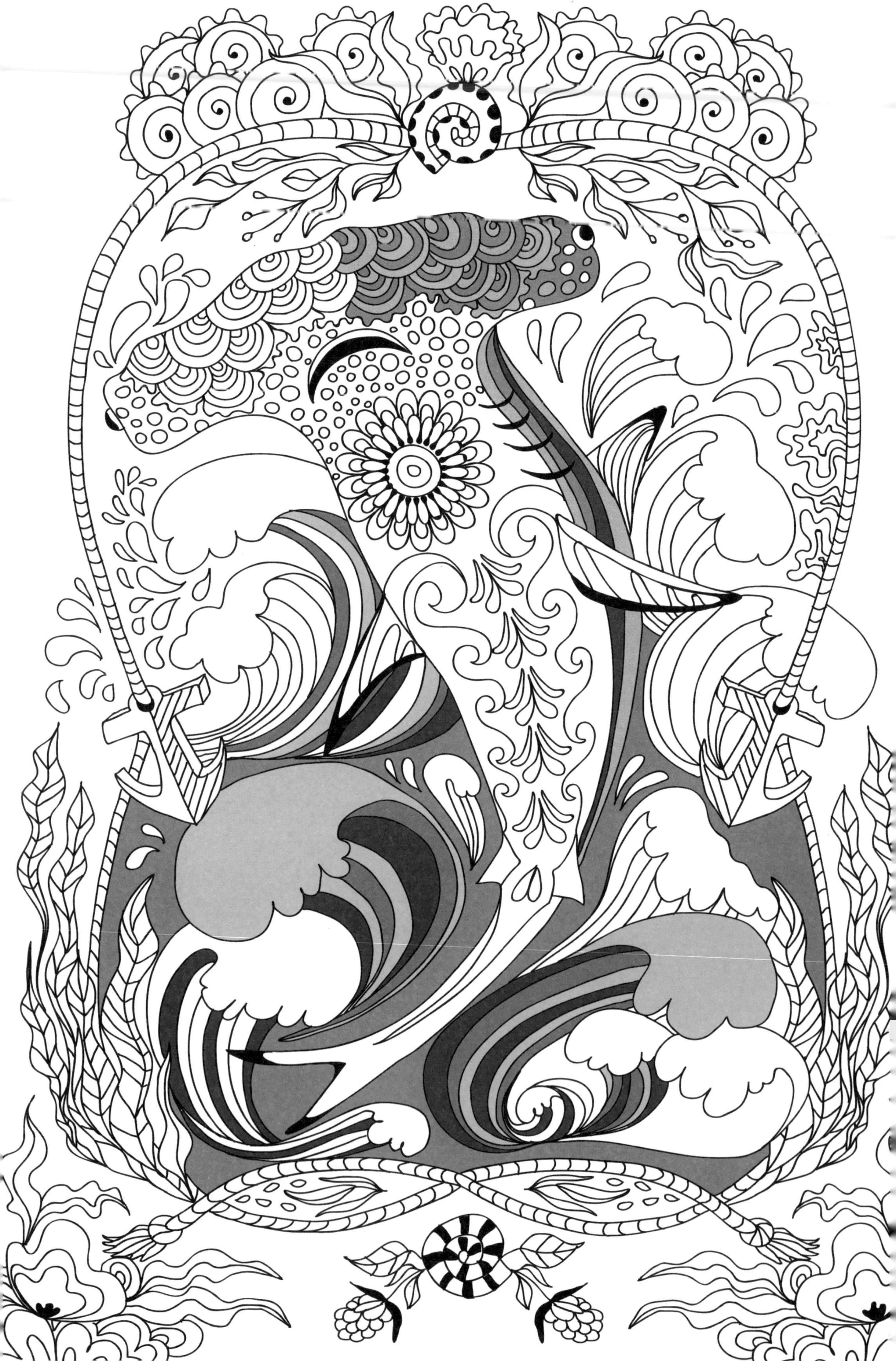

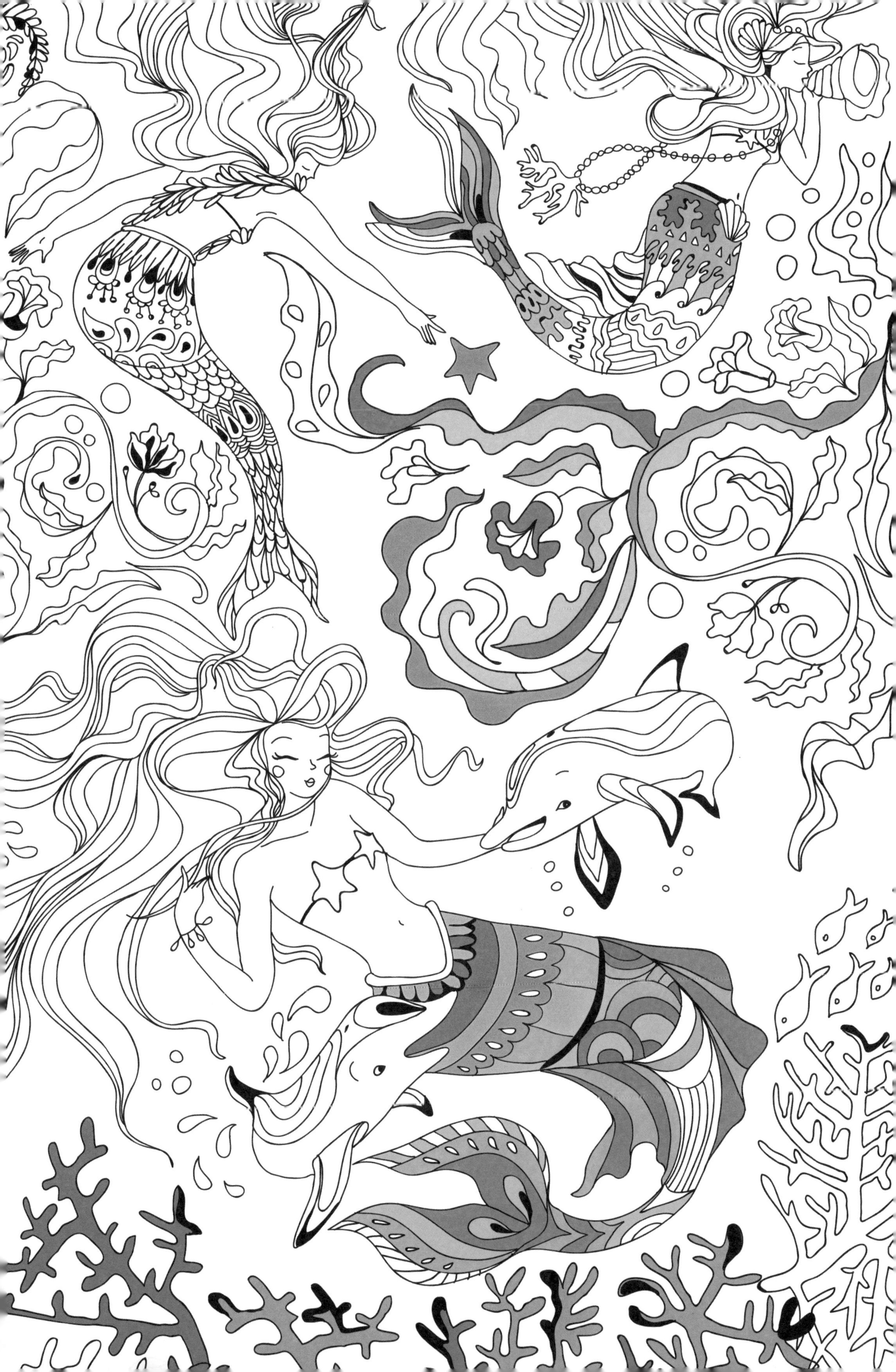

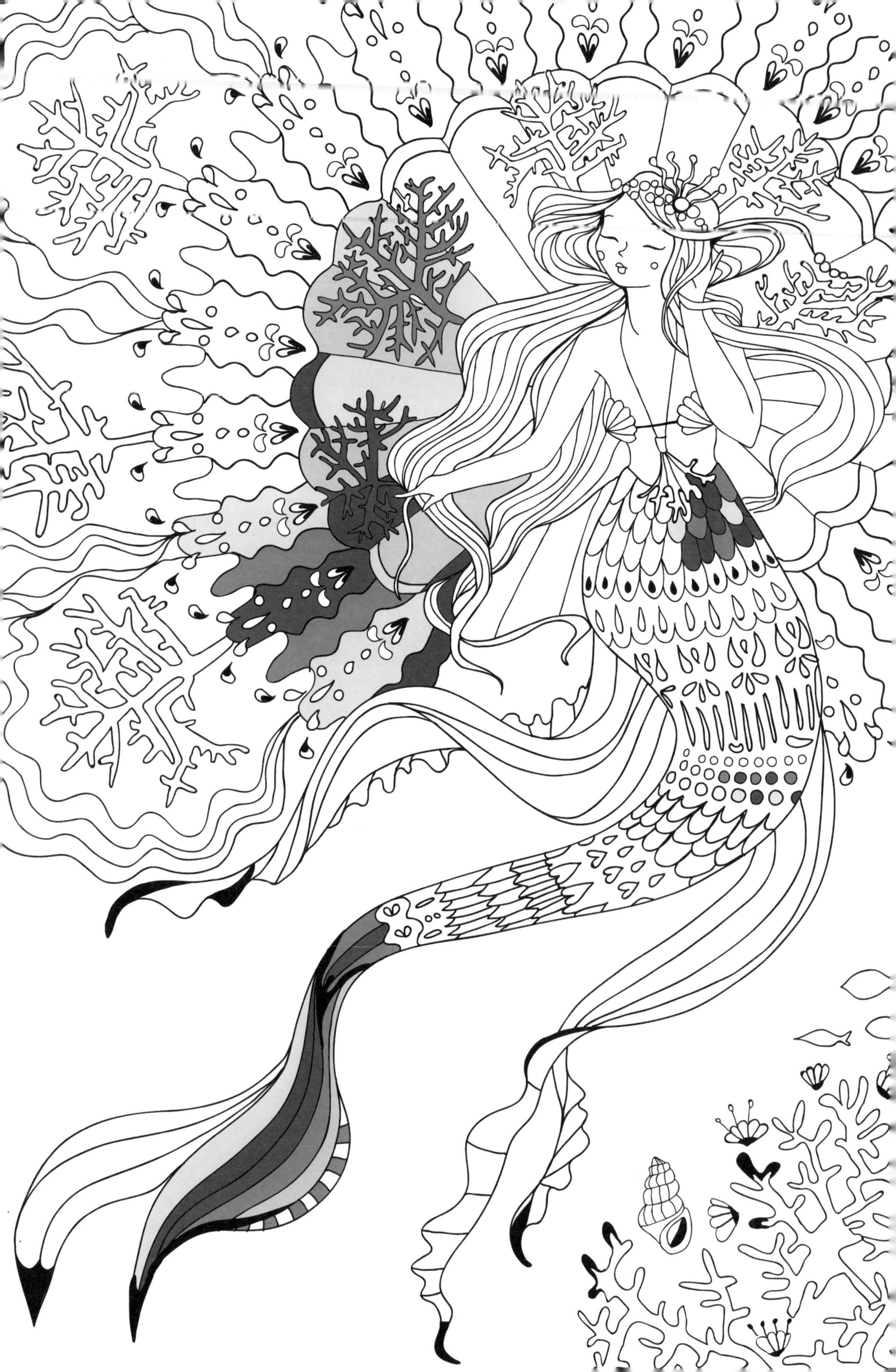

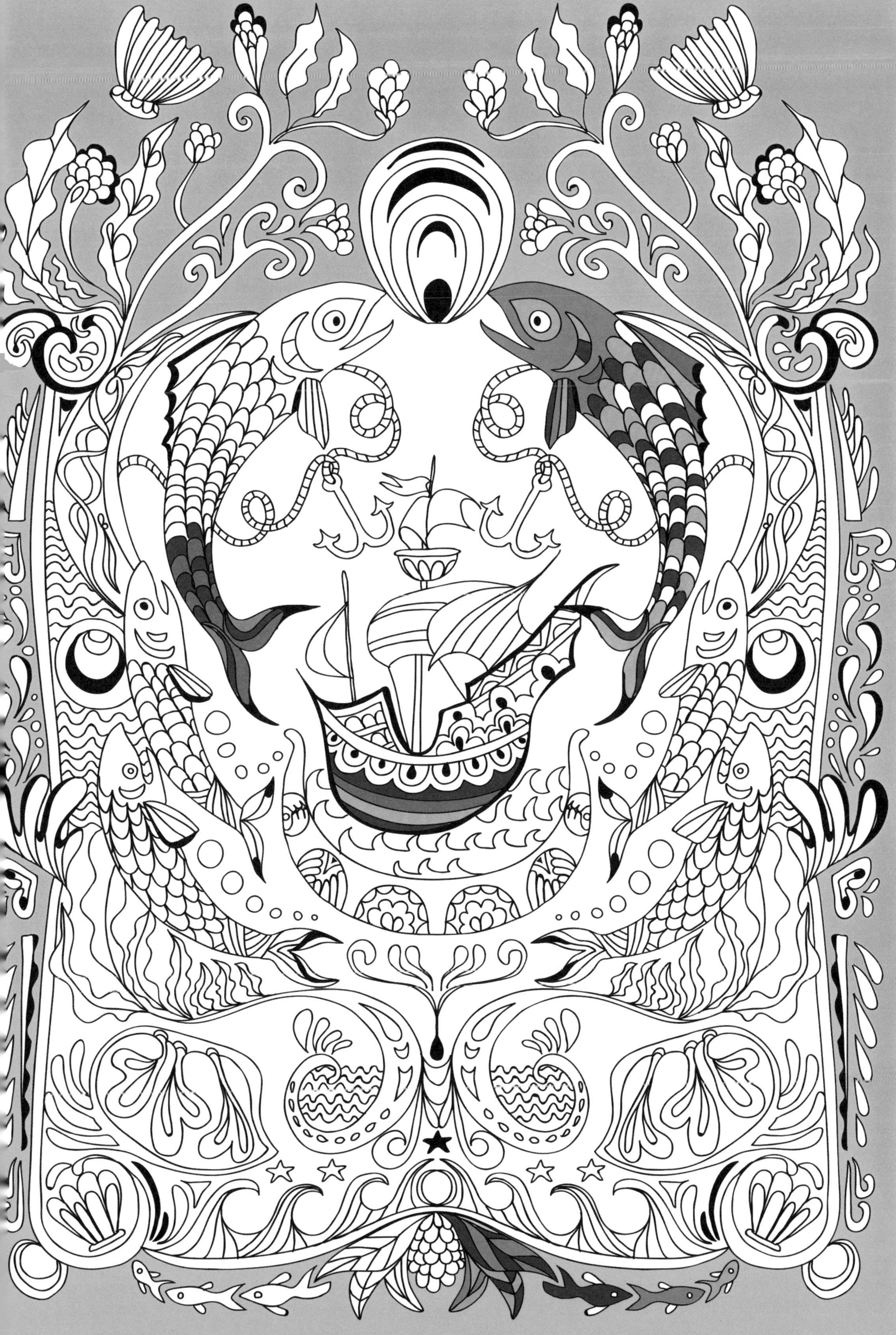

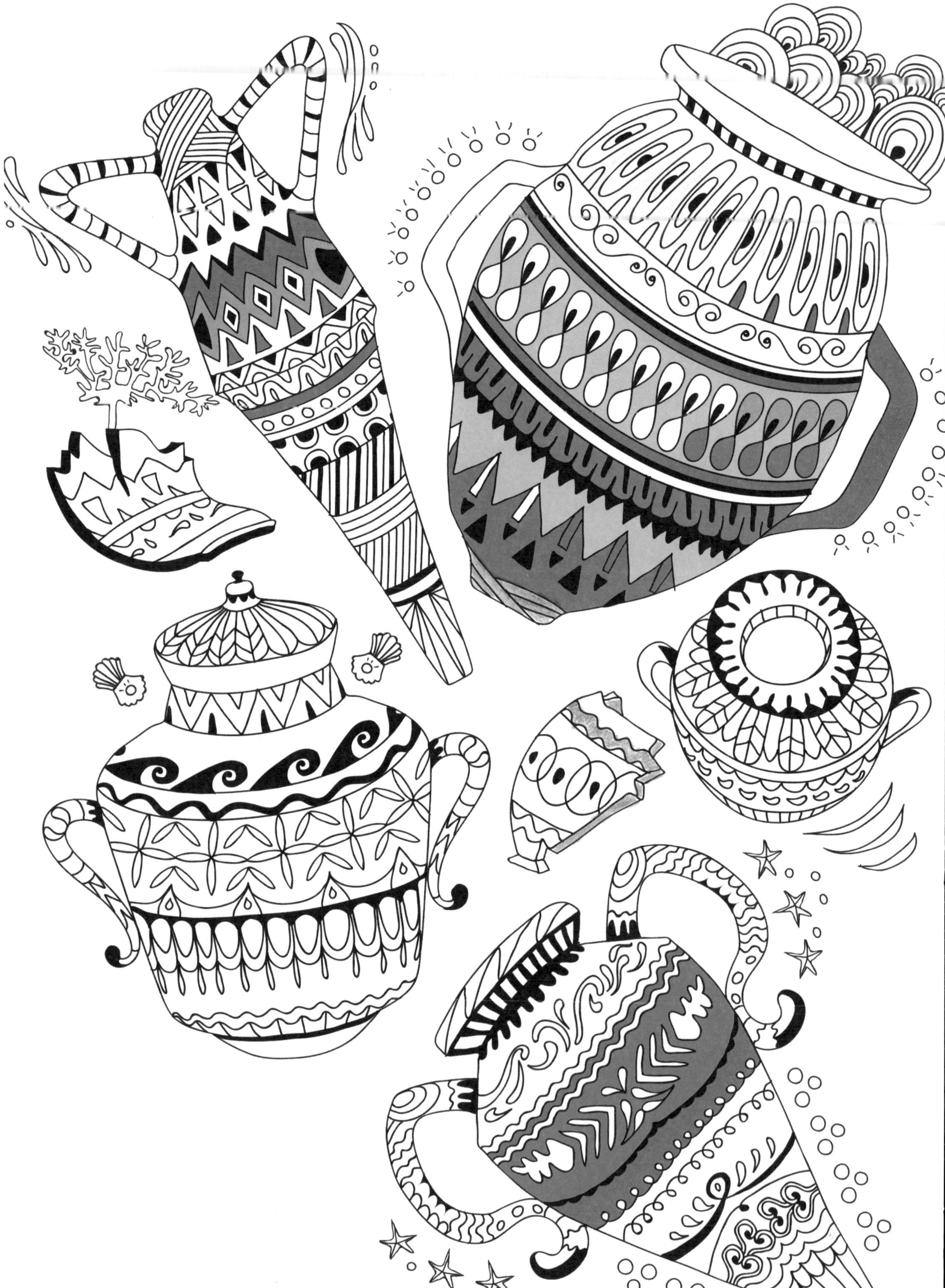